Jan. 30th 2016

Mary...
anything I'm here.
is possible if
you want it bad
enough

Love,
[signature]

My book is dedicated to my Parents:

James Latour Johnson & Rhonda Anne Payne-Dugan

&

Grandparents:

William Henry Payne & Betty Jean Payne

Clarence Benjamin Alexander & Dora Mae McLemore

In loving memory of my father *James Latour Johnson*, how I wish I could move back the hands of time…just to tell you not to worry about me, and that I finally found my way. Daddy, had I known then, what I know now…I wouldn't have allowed anyone to take me away from those who loved me the most. You needed me, and I failed you. I write this book in your honor, hoping to show other women, that no man comes before family. Continue resting in eternal peace.

Paying Homage…

The very first book I ever wrote was when I was in the 3rd grade, that book was entitled "My mother is a race car driver," I'll never forget how impressed my teacher was and how elated her praises made me feel. I have carried that feeling with me for over 20 years and early on I realized that I had the ability to move people thru my words. This experience has been eye opening and overwhelmingly joyful and has allowed me to become yet more aware of the woman I was and the woman that I am still striving to be.

I am by no means an expert on love, drugs, or prison but I am an expert on how to survive and to get out of your own way so that the pain doesn't become unnecessary suffering. There is a tremendous difference. You cannot control the pain that comes in your life. You can control how long that pain effects your life. There are so many people along the way that have helped make my dreams possible and supported my decision to tell my story. For those people I am truly thankful, because you gave me strength on those days when I questioned my own existence and could not find anything to be happy about.

Words could never fully express the gratitude I have for people believing in me and me genuine love. I have carried many fears with me along the way and thru my writing I have learned, that I am not alone in the fear of never being truly loved, being addicted to drugs, being a victim of domestic violence and fighting to just feel normal. Thru my addictions there has been that one invisible force that carried me and kept me from death and that is God. I prayed to him many, many nights. Some prayers were answered and some were not. Now, I know why some weren't.

To my mother who never once turned her back, even when she should have, also has my eternal gratitude. The love we share is special. Without you, I could have very well been dead. Thank you for supporting me both emotionally and financially. Thank you for convincing me that I am worthy. To both of my grandmothers, thank you for taking me in when I was using and abusing everyone and everything around me. I thank you. To my sisters and brothers thank you for allowing me to be the little sister. When I should have been the big sister and couldn't. I apologize for not showing you a better way to live. To my Uncle Ronald Alexander thank you for being a father figure. As well as, my friend, my confidant and for fighting battles that I should have been fighting myself.

To my Aunt Carol Simmons-Johnson I appreciate every talk we had and every piece of advice you have ever given me.

I have so many wonderful friends that have played a pivotal role in my transformation from victim to survivor. I appreciate you in ways that bring tears to my eyes. To the following people: thank you for loving me, guiding me, giving me tough love, allowing me to cry on your shoulder, and turning from friends to family. Your loyalty cannot be surpassed... Marlana Williams, Roma Marie Young, Takesha Polk, Mayalia Barries, Teekie –Shalanna Scott, Eddi P, Marlon Lewis, Rahsaan Ferguson, Greg Wright, Chris Johnson, Jana Hierl, Stevenson Fisher, Charla Peterson, and Mary Moran. A very special Thank You to Cindy Mendonca, without your laptop this project would have been seriously delayed. Thank you for helping me, finish this. You have become an amazing friend to me. As well as a special thank you to LeGrecia Parker, for your help with my "Sip & Sign," book signing party.

There are also two very special bosses in my life that believed in me and gave me second chances; Steve Pirotta and Cindy Robins, thank you for being much more than the people who signed my paychecks. You believed in me and allowed me to improve my work ethics.

I picked up a few folks along the way that also had a creative part in this process. Or gave me a platform to tell my story; Dimitri Jenkins, Erk tha Jerk, Kisha N. Jones, Urban Rock Tee Shirt, Christopher Randolph, Lyvell James of "Chabot College Radio Station," Leon DNas Sykes of "The Streets is Talking" Radio Show, "Lucky Dollaz" of Chabot College Radio Station, Ramon Smith of the "44 Restaurant & Bar, and Eltonette Harris– "World Wide Women's Group -Her Story."

Also, to my followers via social media who have... hit the like button, double tapped, retweeted, or in-boxed me your support has also been pivotal in my journey. I appreciate everyone whether your name is above or not, your support has been a significant factor in my life as well.

This book will be amazing because that is my destiny. I hope that you enjoy every page and you are inspired to:

"Create a Life Worth Living."

This photo was taken during, my very first interview with Lyvell James (Chabot College Radio Station) and one of my graphic designers Dimitri Jenkins; both of them have played an enormous role in the success of my book. I was so nervous but Lyvell made me feel right at home. Then I look out into the lobby and I saw that Dimitri had come to support me. Over these last few months, Dimitri has played a huge role in a lot of creative decisions. As well as he has become a good friend, that makes me smile on days that I am overwhelmed. I am very thankful to have them both in my life.

This photo was taken during, my second interview on the show, "The Streets Is Talking," with DNas. I reached out to him on social media regarding appearing on his show and he showed me nothing but love. He did advise me that he generally only featured musicians on his show, but when I sent him the reason behind my request and shared some of my story he was more than willing to help. I am very appreciative of the connections I have made, that turned into friendships.

There is a lot to be said about Erk Tha Jerk. This photo was taken the first day that I met him. He was appearing on the same radio show that I was. I remember being so nervous, that I spilled a glass of water all over the counter. He is an amazing artist. I was very fortunate to be able to work with him. He captured exactly what was needed in all of my photo shoots. In my opinion his artistry and creativity have yet to be surpassed. Erk's artistry reaches beyond the scope of being a rapper or a photographer. He is an artist in every aspect of the word. I am thankful for the opportunity, to have worked with someone whose passion inspires me.

Foreword

She is **Ne Plus Ultra** *(perfection: the highest level of excellence, or something that reaches it.)* I am not humbled by anything except my children and parents. I am in great gratitude to her. I wish to one day see her spirit grow to the size of a universe.

Pierre Goldstein

Time Only Gets Better From Here

Just when you think all is cursed

And your spirit feels like it's part of the earth

Someone has a hold of you heart, mind, body and soul

Such an icy grip that your world turns cold

You forget who loves you, and those who cared

We always called to remind you that the love was still there

To be afraid to leave him to us…. this was untrue, unreal

We had no idea you lost control

At loves wheel

There was no way this man could love you more than we do

We would never send you anywhere, with your eye black and blue

But no tellin' *what love will make you do*

It might even make you sit down a year or two

To really reflect on what you had REALLY been through

Time to think… gave you time to grow

The way you smile now, no one would ever know

The pain that you suffered from…

Instead you inform them….that it only gets better from here

Time only gets better from here

Jasmine Marie Johnson

I knew that I had to tell my story. In hope of saving someone else's life.

LOVE MADE ME DO IT

BY

MS. TAMEKIA NICOLE

TABLE OF CONTENTS

CHAPTER 1

LOVE AT FIRST SIGHT

Tamekia Nicole

I'll never forget the night that I fell in love. There is just something wonderful about being in love. I was not prepared to experience love at first site. This night was like no other, I met the man that I would spend the next 10 years with. Go to the bottom with, but never make it to the top with. I would be shown the depths of hell, and realize the limits that love should have.

We met on October 22nd 1999. I loved him instantly, smitten by his charm, and his sarcastic sense of humor. But at that time I didn't know what I would be sacrificing. I didn't know that my freedom, sanity, and my life would be put on the line. Willingly, I put him before all others. There was no forewarning that our ideas of love were polar opposites. Looking back I believe that it was all worth it, if I save someone else from making similar mistakes. Allow my story to give you not only a choice but a voice... I lived thru the abuse, the drugs, the incarceration and the ultimate betrayal. Initially, I wanted to experience the greatest love of my life. However, I experienced something much better. I learned how to survive and keep going. Our 1st encounter was a little out of the ordinary. I was practicing for my driver's license test, with a friend of mine. But we took a detour. This detour delivered me to my lovers door step. His brother answered the door, invited us to come in and make ourselves comfortable. His brother disappeared into a back room. I overheard him say, "Blood, wake-up there is some fine light skin girl in the living room with an S Curl." I tried hard not to laugh. I was curious to see who would come out of the back room.

What an entrance he made. He was tall and handsome with a big smile plastered on his face. He looked me up and down. Then looked at the engagement ring on my finger and started laughing. He started singing…. "Engage me baby, crescent jeweler baby." "Whoever gave you that ring should be ashamed of their self." I tried not to laugh, as I glanced down at my hand. He was right my fiancé should have been ashamed of his self. For many reasons not just the size of my ring. He broke the ice with his jokes and he had my attention. We mingled; me and him and his brother and my girlfriend. We laughed, drank and talked shit. I was young, wild and carefree, and open to any possibility that could bring happiness. We moved into the dining room and played dominoes. I sat across from him and I remember being nervous. He never took his eyes off of me. Usually, I am never nervous and very clever, with plenty to

2

Tamekia Nicole

say. I kept trying to search for the right words. So I blurted out, "This isn't an S Curl by the way."

Right at that moment no-one else seemed to be in the room. That must be the moment I fell in love. He laughed at my outburst. We joked like we knew each other for years. That familiarity pulled me in and turned me on. It seemed like we sat there forever. Flirting & laughing. I wanted to touch him. Our feet kept touching under the table making me wonder if his skin was soft. There was definitely sexual chemistry in the air. With no warning, I slid my foot up his pant leg. His skin felt soft. He looked surprised at how forward I was. I just smiled and kept on playing. I've always been the type to get my way. I've always been the type to seek instant gratification, tonight was no different. I had no concerns or desire to go home. My only desire was to kiss him and feel his body next to mine. As the night carried on, he made it clear that he desired the same from me.

I followed him into his bedroom. He kissed me and held me. I moaned and kissed him back. When our lips parted I asked him a simple question. "Do you practice safe sex?" "Yeah" "Well let's practice some." My lover pleased me. The sexual gratification was overwhelming at first. My body had never experienced multiple orgasms. My fiancé had never made me feel like this. I knew that this was more than just a one night stand. Chemistry has an ability to change lives and I wanted it to change mine. I had every intention on being with him. Unfortunately, I still had some other unfinished business to tend to. My fiancé. I left my lovers place in the wee hours of the morning. I could barely talk. All I could do was giggle. During the drive back to my house, panic started to kick in. I had some serious explaining to do as to where I had been. I was relieved to see that no one was home. I saw a note on the fridge "I stepped out, don't wait up." Which wasn't unusual, at least he left a note this time.

So my girlfriend and I relished in our escapades of the night before. As apprehensive as I was to share, I did what we all do with our friends. I dished the details. In great detail I told her how many times, he made me say yes please. I told her that I begged him not to stop and he complied. My heart pounded as I retold my conquest. She was hanging on my every word. So was my fiancé. When I finished my story he exposed his hiding place. My pantry door slid open. My fiancé, was toting his bible, and smoking a Newport. There was a deadly silence in the room. There was nothing that I could say, that would make this situation better.

Tamekia Nicole

I was exposed. My girlfriend lunged for the door. He stopped her and made her sit down. He grabbed me and threw me down. I knew better than to get back up. There would be no point I was powerless against him.

My fiancé stayed quiet for a moment. Before he demanded that we take him to the liquor store. He drank until he passed out. The coast was clear. My girlfriend was free to leave and so was I. I stepped over my fiancé's limp body and dialed my lover's number. I need him to come and get me before round two started.

I jumped in his car. I didn't even look back. I slid down in the passenger seat, terrified that my fiancé would see us. No words were spoken on the drive back to his house. I was at a loss for words. Thankfully it was a short ride to my lover's house. The look on my face must have spoken volumes. "You can lie down if you want." "You look exhausted." I smiled and nodded. He snuggled up next to me. I readjusted my position so that I could lie on his chest. I felt so safe in his arms. I inhaled. This felt right. This is where I wanted to be. I loved the way he felt, and the way he smelled. How his bottom lip was tucked under his top lip ever so slightly. He slept and I tried to sleep. I had too many things on my mind. Then I gave up and just watched him. It was serene. I needed that serenity.

I woke him up a few hours later and asked him to take me home. I could tell that he didn't want to. I didn't want to leave him. But I needed to go home and deal with my fiancé. Unlocking my front door was terrifying. Especially, since I had no idea what would be on the other side. My fiancé was wide awake. He looked at me with so much disgust. The anger that was on his face paralyzed me. He bombarded me with questions, "Is he bigger than me?" "Did you like it?" "Did you kiss him?" "Did you suck his dick?" I tried to remain silent. How was I supposed to answer those questions? This was too much.

I know I was wrong. But I was also aware that our relationship was not perfect. He continued to drill me. Finally I gave in. "Yes, he made me climb the walls!" "That's what you wanted to hear right?" "He has everything you don't have." "Now leave me alone before I really hurt your feelings." My fiancé started to cry. So I shut up. I said enough. The damage was done. Although I was at fault, I would not allow him to continue this physical and verbal abuse. Finally, he stopped talking. My

Tamekia Nicole

house had become a war zone. I was walking on egg shells around him. Too scared to talk to him or even look in his direction. I knew that if I said the wrong word. He would hurt me. The days and nights flew by. I hadn't had one opportunity to talk to my lover. That was killing me.

I thought about him every day. Nevertheless, I never felt that it was safe to call him. My fiancé was watching me like a hawk. Until I just couldn't take the separation anymore. My lover had my attention. Hell, he had my heart. I started calling him from work, the BART Station, even payphones at the grocery store. I met up with my lover on several occasions. Meeting up with him was definitely dangerous. But it was worth it just to see his face. Ironically, on the days that we did have an opportunity to see one another, my fiancé would inspect me. He would look to see if the back of my hair was matted down. He even wanted to inspect my panties. But what he really wanted; was for me to tell him what he already knew. My cheating was evident and obviously much more than just sex. I was happy with my lover and miserable with my fiancé. My lover invaded every inch of my being. My soul. My thoughts. He gave life to me.

I spent countless hours mapping out, how I could see him without getting the shit beat out of me. I was home alone and didn't have a clue where my fiancé went. The timing couldn't be any more perfect. I called my lover and suggested that we have movie night. "I'm already dressed." "I'll meet you out front in 10 minutes." That was all that needed to be said. I walked to the front of my complex and waited for my lover to pull up. I surveyed the area. I didn't see my fiancé or anything suspicious. Finally, I would have the opportunity to relax. I heard my lovers car, before I seen it turn the corner. I stood closer to the curb and he pulled up and opened up my door. As soon as I sat down, my fiancé leaped out of yet another hiding place. The bushes. He wanted to fight me. Instead, my lover was ready to fight him. I was caught up, between my past and my future.

Violence wouldn't solve this situation. I didn't want anyone to get hurt. I told my lover that I would be okay. I wanted to do whatever it took for my fiancé, to thoroughly understand that it was over. We needed to have a heart to heart. I needed to be honest about my feelings. He was belligerent and loud. I was ushered into the house. This was not going to go well. He hit me so hard in my throat that I gasped for air. Once again

5

Tamekia Nicole

I was down on the ground. But this time I got back up. He put me in a backwards choke hold. Covering, my nose and mouth. He pinned me down to the ground. With his body weight anchoring me down, I started feeling dizzy. If I didn't get away, he was going to kill me. The thought of dying gave me the strength I needed.

I managed to reach the front door. He was right behind me. He grabbed the back of my shirt, making it rip from my body. But that didn't stop me. I pushed thru the darkness like the devil was on my heels. I was calling out for help. A neighbor heard me and let me in. "Please, let me use your phone!" I was half naked from the waist up and out of breath. I covered up my chest and dialed my lover's number. He answered. "Please bring me a tee shirt and meet me in the back." A few minutes later, my lover was there. He hugged and held me. "Are you ok?" "I am now." My lover made me feel so comfortable. He never asked what happened. But I'm sure he knew. I was thankful that he came and saved me. I didn't have any concerns about my fiancé finding me. We ordered pizza and put in a movie. I was trying to put everything out of my head and relax. Then the phone rang, and rang, and rang a few more times. I loved the fact that he was so into me and not his phone. Then that damn phone rang one more time. This was the ring that was heard around the world.

He jumped up to go get it. He listened for a moment, and then waved me to the phone. All I heard was my ex's slurred speech thru what sounded like spit bubbles. "Do you love her?" "Are you with her right now?" Then he yelled "give me back my girl!" I wanted to laugh. Then I wanted to cry. I took the phone and hung it up. It commenced to ringing while we made love. I didn't want my fiancé anymore. I had lost interest. He would just have to deal with it. It was okay when he cheated. But not when I did? How ironic.

Do I attempt to rectify my relationship? Or do I further indulge in the possibility of a forever situation with my lover? I had a decision that needed to be made. I wouldn't be able to rest easy knowing that I was leaving so many loose ends. I decided the best thing to do was to figure out if my relationship could be fixed. If it couldn't, then I needed to end it properly. So I stopped everything. I stopped calling my lover. I stopped seeing my lover, and I stopped all my emotions towards my lover. I went back to a mediocre existence. I worked and came home. My main focus

Tamekia Nicole

point was repairing my relationship. My fiancé really tried to play his part too. He got a job, made some better friends and curbed his alcohol intake. I loved him enough to give him this opportunity. But truthfully I was scared of him. I was scared that if I did anything wrong he might kill me.

Although our mission to reconnect had been a mutual goal, something was missing. There was no love. That had been replaced with fear. It was a complacent existence. I was just going along, so that no one would be hurt. Physically or mentally. I did my best to play nice, but every second I dreamed of my lover coming to rescue me. Months went by and I continued to ignore calls and pages from my lover. Until, right before New Year's Eve 1999. Our house phone rang with a call from an unknown caller. I picked up and I heard is voice. "Can you talk?" "I can't stop thinking about you." I gasped for air, with my heart pounding. I replied. "I'll call you later." It was back on. I was going to make sure, that it had a better beginning than before. I reflected for a whole week, before I decided to have the conversation with my fiancé. At dinner I told him he should move on. I would give him no more than a month to get everything together and leave. He said ok. A few days went by; we didn't speak, sleep or eat together. It was nice. But really eerie. I couldn't read him.   Literally, I was counting down the days until my fiancé would be out of my life. I had recently picked up extra hours, mostly on Saturday's, to keep myself out of the house. This Saturday would be like no other. I came home happy. I had plans with my lover later that day. I just needed to stop at home first. Walking up to the front door of my apartment, I noticed that something was off. My front door was slightly ajar. I nudged it open with my foot and what a sight I seen. My fiancé was lounging in the recliner, in his boxers. He looked like a deranged maniac. I gave a simple smile; "Bitch I feel like killing you." Was his response.

I dragged the house phone to the porch and called my sister. I was going to need somewhere to sleep for the night. She didn't answer. I knew all too well, that he was dangerous.   This wouldn't be a fair match no matter what. So I left. I went to my neighbor's house…the pastor and his wife. Hopefully their house could be a temporary safe haven. They fed me and prayed for my situation. Nightfall was upon us and I decided that it was safe to go home. Walking down the pathway to my apartment, I seen Fire Marshalls, E.M.T's and Police Officers! Shaking my head I was terrified to see what lie on the other side of my front door. Every bit of clothing that I owned had been doused with a bottle of Christian Brothers Cognac and lit on fire. What used to be my living room was now an extinguished bon fire.

Smoke damage every-where, with a gaping hole in the living room floor. Everything was either covered in soot or burned to a crisp. I stepped out looking towards the parking lot, and saw my fiancé. Partially dressed in the back of the ambulance, I kept thinking I was dreaming. My first apartment on my own, up in smoke literally… My sanity was on the brink of destruction. All the material items that burned weren't my concern. Following my heart was. Talking with the police officers, I realized that they were just as clueless as I was. They said they would charge him with arson and I would be notified prior to his release from the local jail. Three days later he was out. All charges dropped. I received an automated call advising me that he was released. My heart dropped. I was petrified wondering what would happen next.

Those three days I had spent cleaning, scrubbing and trying to figure out what I was going to wear to work. Since everything I owned was now gone. He didn't come back to our charbroiled apartment immediately. So I just waited, and waited. On that 2nd night after his release, I heard the faintest cry around 1:30 in the morning. I looked out my bedroom window and didn't see anything. Then I looked out the kitchen window still nothing or anyone in sight…then I looked onto the patio and there he was crying his eyes out. The smell of liquor was so pungent it seeped into the house thru the sliding glass door. What I used to feel towards him had vacated. I couldn't even imagine ever being turned on by him. The sight of him made me sick.

He made me wish things that you should never wish on anyone, not even an enemy. I told him to get the fuck off of my patio. He slithered off that patio into the night, wearing a withered pair of hospital scrubs. The next day I put his belongings in a box. Called his mama and asked her to come get his shit. She was also tired of him and I damn sure was tired of him. This relationship had run its course. Everything was devalued and deflated. Especially me. His alcoholism took over his rationale and our relationship. I refused to be destroyed any further. As if it couldn't get any worse. I came home from shopping to a three day eviction notice on my door.

Tamekia Nicole

I tried to clean up and really get things back together without anyone being too suspicious of what had taken place. But seriously, there was a big gaping burnt hole in the center of my living room. I took my eviction notice with a grain of salt. My life was fucked up. I prayed every night for peace of mind. My lover seemed to be the only way out of this hell that I was still in. Forced out of my apartment, due to my fiancés; lack of control. That was my very first everything on my own, and I lost it. His addiction became my problem too. Luckily I was able to move right into a small studio apartment.

CHAPTER 2

AFTER THE SMOKE CLEARED

Love Made Me Do It

Tamekia Nicole

The first few days I didn't feel comfortable in my new spot so I stayed with my lover. He caressed me at night time when I would talk in my sleep. He soothed my night terrors. He checked my fiancé every time his drunken ass called. His affection never towards me never wavered. I never had to be anyone other than who I was. I was a damsel in distress and he was my knight in shining amour.

My lover and I spent many nights talking; it was so nostalgic and endearing. Those talks meant the world to me. They were open, honest, and full of everything that a wounded soul needed. My lover said that I was the type of woman that would make him clean out his closet and settle down. On a crisp winter night…Not really cold but the air has a slight chill to it. We lie amerced in a magical moment. We were savoring the taste of our new love and each other. We were smitten beyond belief. Then, slowly a new hell began to unravel.

My lover woke up and ran into the living room. I stayed in the bedroom hoping that whatever the commotion he heard was just a stray cat. But of course a stray cat would have been an easy fix. You stomp your foot and the cat will scurry away. But an Ex-Girlfriend who has broken into your house is a little harder to get rid of. A woman who is scorned has sharper claws than an alley cat. I peeked out of the bedroom and seen an attractive woman being ushered by force, out into the backyard. She wanted to see me, wanted to see who took her place. Who lie in his bed? Who kept him intrigued like a love sick little boy. It was me and little did she know that I had no intentions on leaving.

Her unwanted entrance had no effect on me but I saw that it was affecting him. I lie awake that night wondering if all of this was a mistake. I would wait until he brought the situation up to me…To determine an infinite answer. He picked me up from my house a few days later and said that we needed to talk. We sat there in the same dining room where we met and we talked. We talked about what we meant to each other. We talked about how he grew up. I listened as he told me family secrets. How we grew up was an essential ingredient to our failed relationship. There was a lot of dysfunction on both sides. It felt good for my lover to open up to me about such personal things in his life. We were establishing trust. He also went on to tell me how his sister had a bad drug problem and that's how his mom wound up raising her children. Including the one that was conceived with his father.

It was a lot of information to take in. But I was more than happy to take any burden off of this man after all he has already done for me. We also talked about the intruder from the other night. He said that she was crazy and that they had been over. He no longer wanted to be with her, but she didn't get the hint. My lover even showed me where her name was in his phone book, and how it was now scratched out. I told him that I understood and I believed him. Which I did, there was no reason for me to think otherwise.

Our comfort level continued to grow. Every time we were apart I could only think of him. I don't think that my heart ever experienced such a profound feeling of love. It was love in the rawest form. Then it happened... He said it, those three little words. That make your heart skip a beat and your legs tremble... "I love you." Never had those words sounded sweeter than when they parted from his lips. Jokingly, he said that he should take me to Reno and marry me so that I knew he was serious. It was that emotion that I felt like I had searched for my entire life. Knowing that one person was yours. That they belonged to you, I felt like my lover was really mine. Often women will look for signs in a relationship that you are the only one and I was no different. I needed that validation in order to continue to be with him. The 1st of many validations of "his love" came the day he told me I could stay in the bed while he went to work. He trusted me enough to stay at his house alone. I couldn't wait for him to leave so I could begin looking around. Looking for clues and making sure no other woman was in my territory.

I looked around. I opened drawers, emptied pants pockets. I didn't find anything in the places I looked. Then the phone rang. I let the answering machine pick up. The voice that began speaking was so sexy, confident and demanding. It was her. It was his ex. "I just wanted to know if we were still on for lunch today." I was on the edge of his bed listening wondering, what do I do? So I picked up the phone..."Hello?" She hung up. I tried to *69 her back but the number was restricted. I found his phone book where her number had been scratched out and tried to make out the number. But I couldn't. Eventually, I found a phone bill and determined her number by eliminating other numbers. That I knew weren't hers. I finally found her number on the 4th page of an 8th page

Tamekia Nicole

phone bill. I dialed that number with so much emotion, that I had to keep redialing because I was missing the actual numbers. As soon as I heard her voice, "He ain't going to lunch with you today, or any other day." "Matter of fact I'm in his bed right now," then I hung up. The phone rang again. This time when the answering machine picked up; the voice I heard was his. He was not happy at all. Fuck! It was apparent that they still felt some type of way about one another. Whether it was lover or not, was still to be determined. My only job was to prove that I was the keeper. Obviously, he was pissed. "Pick up this damn phone." "I know your right there Johnson pick that phone up." I picked up like I had run to the phone…"Hello, yes….what?" "Yes, we can talk about it when you get home." That was the end of that conversation.

I would just wait until he came home. But in the meantime I was going to continue to look around. Obviously he hadn't totally gotten rid of her completely. Now I needed to see if any other women were still present and accounted for. I searched high and low until I was literally sweating. The last search proved to be very lucrative. I found some unmarked VHS tapes. I watched them all one by one. The 5th tape I watched was the jackpot. My lover was on tape with a very large, very dark woman. It was three of them, her, him and his cousin. They were taking turns having sex with this woman. I put the tape into slow motion so that I could determine the time frame of when this took place. After half an hour of pausing, stopping and rewinding, I noticed a calendar in the background. I was able to see the date. It was about a year or so before he knew me. Perfect! I could care less what he did prior to knowing me. Even though that was a prelude, as to what was to come between me and him. So now I had this tape. I would use the tape to derail his anger, about the phone conversations from earlier.

Finally, I heard him come home. My heart was beating so fast. I thought he would be able to hear it. Here goes nothing, but at the same time here goes everything. I was ready for his questions, lies and accusations. But would he be ready for what I had for him? I doubt it. "Why did you call her?" I said "Why were you having lunch with her today?" He paused. Then I said "Oh yeah, I found this today too." "Care to explain?" I pulled the tape out and popped it into the VCR. I stretched out at the head of the bed in my boy short's. I was going to make it impossible for him to resist me, even in the heat of an argument. I had the remote in my hand, all the while I am thinking *please lover give me a valid*

13

Tamekia Nicole

reason to trust and believe whatever you say. But if I didn't believe him, pressing play will be my only pleasure. I pressed play.

While I was replaying his sexual encounter, he ran out of the room and into the parking garage….Typical man, no ability to explain or defend his actions. When he finally came back into the house we just laughed and laughed! He knew I was a little crazy. But he also knew that I loved him…he said "Only crazy girls have the best pussy and are the most loyal," "What am I going to do with you?" I replied "Love me the right way, or else." He may have been laughing, but I wasn't. I was keeping mental notes on my lover as his actions.

But honestly I think the attraction that other women had towards him was the exact reason why he held my heart for over a decade.

Tamekia Nicole

CHAPTER 3

BATTLE OF THE EXES

Tamekia Nicole

Me and his ex played many childish games to get his attention. Finally, weeks went by and there was no word from her and no sign of her. I was happy about that. But I was suspicious. But in the meantime me and my lover began getting closer. We shared more secrets, dreams and our aspirations. We became inseparable. Everything that we did revolved around each other. It felt good to be wanted, needed and loved. He earned my trust back. Then it all began again. The uncertainty, that comes with fairly new relationships. Me and him we were like clockwork, morning, noon, night. Even in our sleep we were connected. Until I had an eerie feeling that something wasn't quite right. Our relationship was at a nice steady pace and sex was extra good. So either he was cheating or I was paranoid. Every experience we had was orgasmic. Every encounter was sexually charged. Every ounce of me was tantalized with excitement. I didn't want to lose him. But I was far from dumb. Something wasn't right.

I called him and he didn't answer. He called right back and said that he would call me when the game was over. Well right back wasn't until the morning. They say all things will come into the light, when the timing is right. When he called in the morning his conversation was weird. He was hitting mute and hiding background noise from my ears. Everything he said sounded like a lie. First he said he forgot to call me back. Then he said he fell asleep. Then he said he thought it was too late to call me back. I thought to myself, *you're a lying piece of shit*. But instead of revealing what I was thinking. I told him to have a nice day at work and that I loved him. He had no idea what rage was brewing inside of me. I started to get ready for work. But instead I called in sick to work and took a cab to his house. I needed to see for my-self what he was trying to hide.

I had a key that he had given me in case of an emergency. Which I thought I could come and go as I please. As I was coming in, they were coming out. She was so closely behind him I could barely see her frail ass. She wasn't as pretty, as I had once given her credit for. She scurried back to his bedroom. He tried to carry me back to my cab. I tried to break free from his arm. I was screaming at the top of my lungs. "I thought you loved me!" "Why did you eat my pussy last night?" "Why did we do it with no condom?" Anything that was private business I was screaming for everyone to hear it. My lover could not have possibly thought that I would leave that easily. I swear every time I thought that things were

Tamekia Nicole

going good for us. There was always something that was standing in the way. Mostly, it was other women. His ex was not the only one. She was just the only one that was consistently present. I was, a screaming, irate, jealous woman going off at 7am.

I kept asking myself, "Why are you here at the ass crack of dawn, sweatin this man?" But I didn't have a logical answer. Except that I was in love. Love was making me do strange things. It was like I was under a spell. Love was driving my every thought and move. So there I stood in the driveway. He was wrestling to keep a hold of my arm. My lover had such a look of disgust on his face. I knew I had gone too far. The thing with me was, I never seen what healthy intimacy looked like. I never saw a genuine healthy love between a man and a woman. So, all my actions represented that. I acted out simply because I didn't know any better. Finally, I cooled down and allowed my lover to put me back into my cab. He leaned in and put the seat belt on me. He also told me to calm down. "Stop crying, let me handle her." I was instructed to go wait for his call. I did just that. I sobbed silently while the cab drove me home. I tilted my head on the window of the cab. Thinking about him and how much I loved him. *I refused to lose.*

But the question I should have posed to myself is, "Would it really be a loss?" I got out the cab. Wiped my tears and unlocked my front door. I put my phone in the bed with me on high volume. I laid there thinking. My thoughts were interrupted by his call. I glanced at the Caller ID and I saw his name. I answered the phone before it finished the first ring. "I am coming to get you, be ready", I said "ok". He pulled up in his 69 Camaro and I jumped in. We didn't talk on the ride. There was no need he already knew and so did I. This would be a love affair; that would last a lifetime. No matter what he did or what he didn't do. He had my heart and that would always be. I sank down into his leather sectional sofa. He sank down right next to me. He put my legs on top of his lap, shook his head and calmly said, "What is wrong with you?" I started crying. Putting my head down, I stuttered "I love you, and I thought you loved me too." Then he gave me the song and dance. He said that she popped up while he was watching the NBA Playoffs. She too had cried and sang the same song I did.

We, as in me and her, were fools in love, with a fool. My promise from him was that it was over with her. Even though, I heard that before.

Tamekia Nicole

I really needed to know what would be different this time. He also said that, his house key was only to be used with permission from him. So I reached into my pocket and gave it back.

My lover also said that if I ever put his neighbors in his business like that, he wound never fuck with me again. I told him that I had to do something to get his attention. But I would do my best not do that again. I think I actually meant it. When you're in love, it's hard to control yourself. I listened but I didn't hear him. The pounding of my heart was drowning out all logic. I should have stopped it right then. I should have let go. But I couldn't and that was just our 1st year together. How did my heart endure 9 more years of him?

I was truly a slave of love and I would slave harder than my ancestors just to make him see that I was the one. When all the lights go out and the party has quieted down…How long do you hang onto the concept of love and the depths it took you too? Hoping that all your hard work and laboring, will amount to a happy ending. I was always willing to any risks to prove my love and my loyalty. Thinking back on those years, I often question what it was that made me insanely in love with this average, mediocre man. Was it the sex? Was it the cat and mouse? Or was I literally addicted to the power struggle between us? Some may say I was a lost young woman, with daddy and abandonment issues. But I say, I was a lost young woman that burned with the desire, to be loved by another person.

My lover continued to do what it is that he did best, love me and fuck me. It was consistent and dysfunctional. We spent countless nights entangled in a web of lust and broken promises. It all felt so right. My emotions were finally in a stable place and his lies were in order. Life was ok. If I didn't see it, or couldn't prove it, then it never happened and I didn't speak on it. The other women came and went, and I stayed. I cooked, cleaned, and was the epitome of the perfect girlfriend. I was obviously putting forth more effort than him.

I needed to leave. I needed to leave him before I kill him and all these bitches. It was becoming too much to handle. He was taking a toll on my emotional wellbeing. My tank was already on empty. I could not take too much more. I made some phone calls and arranged some things. Arizona would be my next stop. Thinking back it hurts to know that I had

Tamekia Nicole

to uproot myself from everything that I was familiar with. Just to keep from hurting myself and others. In my heart I knew, I needed to be away for him. I need to feel and act different than what I currently was. I couldn't do that here in California.

I gave myself one month to get everything together and tie up all my lose ends. When I decide to do something I do it. When I decided I better leave California before I hurt my love and his bitch. I did everything in my power to support a positive transition for myself. Sporadic, is the perfect word to describe how I function even to this day. Although, I'm getting better, I refuse to ponder situations and weigh out the pros and cons. Sometimes it's too scary to handle. My mind was traveling in a million different directions. I questioned myself and my existence within his world. How could my savior turn into someone that I no longer could trust?

This was a man that thought more so with his dick than with his brain. I was functioning at the lowest level in every other aspect of my life. My whole life was suffering because I couldn't think of anything but him and how to hurt her. She was fucking everything up. But in reality if I hurt her physically or emotionally, I was hurting him. I didn't want to hurt him.So I just moved forward with my plan to move to Arizona. I had family out there and I was ready to start over. First I had to tell my lover. I would give him an ultimatum. Maybe by the grace of God I won't be leaving. I knew I had to handle this conversation with finesse, and from a perspective that he never thought of pertaining to me. Looking back I know now, that you can't make anyone do anything. Especially a man, if they haven't already foreseen it for themselves.

CHAPTER 4

TIME TO PACK

Tamekia Nicole

Making myself comfortable, I tried to contain all the emotions that were building up inside of me. I felt like there was a fire burning inside of me. So, I better open up my mouth before I erupt like a volcano. As soon as we settled in the bed for the night, I said "I'm moving." He just looked at me. I continued, "I'm moving to Arizona." More silence. He turned his back to me and said good night.

I felt hot tears streaming down my face, and I wanted to stop them. But I couldn't. I was crying because of the silence that was now festering in the bed with us. There were no questions. There was no loving gaze into my eyes, only quiet. I turned over carefully, with my back to him. The reassurance that I needed to feel was null and void. So that ultimatum idea I had was irrelevant. The next day was a regular, mundane morning. I climbed over him and hit the snooze button. We made love and we basked in the aftermath of that love. We scurried around for the get ready for work necessities, and he dropped me off at the BART Station. We said our goodbyes with a kiss. The kiss we shared that morning was long, and deep.

I took my time walking up to the train platform. I felt low and unwanted. Maybe I would just ride the train to the farthest destination, and at the end he would be there waiting. Apologizing, for being non-responsive when I told him I was moving, *yeah right*...I felt like I had been stabbed a hundred times with a rusty knife. Now my plan to get to Arizona was more underway than it originally was. There was nothing to keep me here and no one I wanted to stay for. Gearing up to go to Arizona wasn't easy. I had never been on a plane or away from my family. Truth be told, I was scared. But I had painted myself into a corner. I had to be accountable for everything that I said I would do and get it done. No matter if it hurt to do or not. So I made phone calls to my relatives living in Arizona. Hoping they had room for me. They did.

I was living in a studio in Hayward. It wasn't a huge space but it was mine. After my apartment was lit on fire, anything was a blessing. Looking around my studio, and I had to figure out what to sell and what to keep. I glanced down at my hand and I started thinking about how it would have been, if had I married my ex. I still had my ring but I wore it on my opposite hand now. I needed to get rid of that too. I sold my ring to the roommate. I don't really know why but he wanted it. Plus any extra money could be used towards my move.

Love Made Me Do It

Tamekia Nicole

No need to hold on to something that would never be. Since I would be moving in with relatives, I knew that all my furniture needed to go. I sat on my bed debating on whether or not I should really leave.

I quit my job as office manager for a prestigious construction company the week prior. So I really had to proceed with this move. My job was an extra weight lifted off of me. Even without my pending move I wouldn't have been able to take too much more of that job. My boss was a dick. His mouth was sarcastic and his manners were non-existent. Even though I was familiar with being a doormat for men in my life. My boss wasn't going to get away with being disrespectful. I have never been with a man that was considered *soft*, nor had I ever been with a man that was considered a *wimp*. My lover was no different. When I told him, my boss, had addressed me as "fuckin, knuckle-head." That posed a serious problem. An abuser does not like anyone else to have the authority or the ability to abuse their prey. So when my love came to pick me up from work on a Friday, he let my boss have it. My boss nearly shit his pants.

The conversation went something like this…"What's up man?" "You have a problem with my girl?" "Uh, uh, uh, no sir, not at all" "I'm not sure what she told you." "She told me you have a problem with that mouth of yours. " "I thought we cleared that up." My boss glanced over at me. He knew damn well we hadn't cleared shit up. "You better watch your fuckin' mouth, before you get yourself hurt." We got in the truck and burnt rubber out the parking lot. That night we made love. If only we could stay this way forever. He was my perfect peace. This is why I didn't know how to leave. But I knew I had too. So as the time ticked. I prepared myself for what was to come. I arranged an interview over the phone with American Express in Arizona, and proceeded with my packing.

Our routine was still in effect, our love on repeat. A small part of me was dying and yet he had no clue. I wanted to be able to love without incident. I wanted to live and be happy. But with a cheater riding shot gun in my life I didn't have a fair chance. Then it happened; my sign from God. It was Friday night our date night. He went into the store and I stayed in the car. Looking for my favorite CD I found a stack of naked Polaroid pictures. However, in the handful of pictures I looked through, not one was of me. *This bastard did not deserve me.*

Tamekia Nicole

It was three or four, different women. My heart fell outside my body and my breathing slowed. I was defeated. I realized at that moment, love shouldn't hurt. This needed to come to an end. Love isn't about betrayal. It's about feeling worthy to another human being. I hadn't found that because, I had yet to know that I was worthy without a man. He was bringing my property value down and I allowed him too. He walked back to the truck, with paper bag full of liquor. I'm sure my face told how I felt. "Just take me home," he looked over at me puzzled, puckering up for a kiss. I repeated, "I am not kidding, take me to my fuckin house." He did just that.

When he stopped in front of my house I threw those Polaroid's in his lap. Crying and hyperventilating, I got my ass out of that truck. I cried myself to sleep. Hoping not to wake up, begging not to feel pain. Asking God what did I do to deserve this treatment? God had given me plenty ways out. I just never chose them. Now am I completely aware that the whole duration of the relationship, I always had my free will. My phone rang and rang and rang, thru- out the night. In the morning I woke up with a new lease on life. I finished packing and had an impromptu yard sale. I couldn't wait to get the fuck out of California. My plane ticket was purchased. My bags were packed, and my love life was on the brink of extinction. But most importantly I needed to get away. I needed to clear my head. I needed to do something different and experience something different in an element that was different.

My love and I were on speaking terms, but I just couldn't understand why he insisted on having more than one woman. Wasn't I enough? Didn't I satisfy him? The answers he gave me over the years would fluctuate from the truth to unbelievable lies. But soon enough, I would put all those issues behind me. It would be wheels up and everything would slowly evaporate behind me. I was looking forward to leaving him and his lies During that last week in California so many things were going on around me. At 22 years old I felt so lost. My maternal grandfather was dying with his mistress by his side. It seemed like everything I was familiar with was slowly parting from my grasp. Two days before I left for my new home in the desert. I went to the hospital to hug, kiss and say goodbye to my grandpa as he lay dying.

It was September 29th, 2001. I carried the guilt of leaving my love behind. Plus leaving my granny and my mother during their time of

Tamekia Nicole

grieving. My grandparents had long divorced but my granny was old school, she stood by his side even when he was undeserving. I watched as him and my granny started parting ways. Acting less, like husband and wife and more like roommates.

Family is important. It's the most important relationship on earth. Granny adhered to that, until my grandpa gave her a reason to proceed with a divorce. After over 30 years of marriage. I sat in the hospital waiting room... me, mama, and granny. His mistress in the waiting room, life seemed to be out of sorts in every which way. I reflected for a moment on my family. My family as I knew it began to take a different shape. Now we all sit separately waiting for the inevitable, for my grandpa to pass onto the next life. Yeah I needed to go. I didn't want to be the strength for everyone else anymore. I wanted to live for just me, just this once. Grandpa passed the next day. Even though I was sad, in two days I would be leaving behind my grief and pain. My life still had to carry on. We made up for the sake of me leaving. I refused to hear the lies about the Polaroid pictures. Or the excuses of why his dick was constantly in between legs that were not mine. I just wanted to have fun and avoid arguing. That night we went to his cousin's house...That night I was introduced to drugs.

I'm talking about Rick James, Whitney Houston, rock and roll type of drugs. Of course I had seen drugs before. My parents came from the Dope Era. I was an 80's baby. I had already seen a lot and was about to experience more. At his cousin's house we drank and reminisced about the course of what our relationship had been. We smothered our liver in alcohol and laughed and enjoyed the night. While a blunt was rolled in another room, I was in the midst of enjoying the night. All the bad times were almost behind me. I sat on his lap and whispered in his ear. "I love you."

He was my lover and always would be. When the blunt was passed to me, no one told me what was in it. But the thickness of the smoke and the sweet scent told me that it was laced. We went back to his house and made love to Mary J Blige. I cried with every stroke. I couldn't help but wonder if this would be our last time together. I was high, he was high...we were *high*. The next day would be high on a plane. With no expectations or knowledge of what was to come. You hope for the best but expect the worst, always. I lay there knowing that in just a few hours I

Tamekia Nicole

would be boarding a plane and embarking on a new journey. I looked to my right and my lover lay so sound, looking so peaceful. I just stared at him for a moment....looking at him and admiring his face. I noticed lines in his forehead that I had never seen before. I let the sleeping giant lay. Finally I fell asleep too. Before I knew it, it was morning. I slipped out of bed and into the shower. It was show time.

He was wide awake when I came out of the shower. I kissed him on the forehead. "Get ready, we still have to go by my sister's house." It was October 1st 2001. It should have been chilly outside but we were having an *Indian summer,* in the Bay Area. The sun was slowly getting ready to set and I was riding shotgun in his truck, music turned up with my hand on his thigh. We hit the freeway and we were on our way to my sister's house so that I could say my goodbyes. So many thoughts ran thru my mind on that short drive. The main one was self-doubt, but I pushed those thoughts out. I needed to do this, and I was going to do this.

My love and I sat in my sister's living room just "shooting the shit" and passing the time. This was good, because I didn't want this goodbye to be emotional. Anything I could do, to prevent a flood of crocodile tears would work best for everyone. But as the time ticked on and minutes passed by, I started to get emotional. Then it was time. We hugged, we kissed, and we said I love you. Making promises to call as soon as I landed safely. It was sad. But I had to leave. I was in too much emotional turmoil. The trip to the airport was lightning fast, we didn't run into any traffic...all systems were a go.

We parked in the lot and when he took his key out of the ignition, he placed his hand on my thigh. I couldn't face him so I looked blankly out my window. Tears fell down my face. I wiped them and jumped out the truck. I stood there for a moment with my back against the passenger side door. I looked up to the sky. Praying to God that my lover to ask me to stay. I walked around the truck and helped him with my luggage. Our eyes met. He grabbed my wrist and pulled me into him. I burrowed my face into his arms. I let my tears flow freely and to my surprise he did too.

There are many pivotal points in a relationship, and outwardly expressing emotions was one. He wiped his face after he lifted his head from my shoulder. But not before I saw him for who he should always represent...a man that was down for his woman. A man, that loved his

Tamekia Nicole

woman. "I love you" "When are you coming back?" "I love you too, but I can't come back until I'm better." "I won't come back until I know that other people can't easily control my emotions." Then in a half whisper I said, "I don't want to go." Either he didn't hear me or didn't care. Then as quickly as the emotions came, they left. We had come to the end of the road. The end of the craziness, he couldn't go any further into the airport with me. One last hug, one last kiss and one last I love you. As I re-tell this story, my eyes tear up thinking about what could have been and why it wasn't.

I swear to God I wanted things to be different between us. I wish that I would have had the wisdom then that I do in life now. The end result may have been different. As I walked with my carry on, I really thought he would come running thru the airport screaming my name. Begging me not to leave, but that never happened. Instead I stood in a trance hypnotized by my own fantasy. Forcing myself to move forward, I boarded the plane. Walked all the way to the back, and sat by the window. I cried until we took off. I was scared. My heart was shattered and my faith had been crushed.

CHAPTER 5

ARIZONA

Tamekia Nicole

I nodded off and when I woke up I was in Arizona. I was so slow getting off the plane. So slow, that the attendants asked me if I needed to be escorted in a wheelchair. This was harder than I imagined.

I shook that feeling off and put a little pep in my step and a smile on my face. I was ready to greet my family. It was so heartwarming to receive such love from my aunt, cousins, and uncle. I hadn't seen them in a very long time. On the ride down the unfamiliar freeway, I cried silently. I honestly didn't know what I was doing. It felt like I was acting like I had my life together. Like I had all the answers, but God knows that the truth. I could barely function. My heart was so hurt, and so broken. I needed the quickest remedy to mend it. I was going to be living in a house with my uncle, my aunt and my four little cousins. I would have to suck up my emotions or else I would be answering a lot of questions from impressionable minds. They went to church at least three times a week. I would be expected to do the same. It's not something I really was in the mood to do. But I knew that nothing else had worked so let me try and reconnect with Jesus. Can't go wrong with Jesus right?

That first night in a new house was eerie. It wasn't uncomfortable, it was just unfamiliar. I called my lover as soon as I was settled. HIs roommate answered the phone. He said that since my lover came back from the airport he was locked up in his room. "Well knock on his door and let him know that I am on the phone, please." My lover picked up the adjacent phone. "Hi baby" and I cried back "Hi baby!" I think that was one of the very first times he called me baby. I sat in my new room at the edge of my bed listening to his voice. He asked me, how my plane ride was. "Bumpy, I cried myself to sleep" "Then I woke up in Arizona." He told me that everything would be ok. "Do you still love me?" I replied "I will never stop, not even death could keep me from it," he sighed... then I sighed. "I love you too"

Drifting in, and out of sleep, I had strange dreams. It was dreams of my lover and her. The frail ex that loved him just as much as I did. I woke up in a cold sweat. Out of habit, when I saw that it was 6am, I picked up the phone and called my lover. Even though I was in another state it was imperative to keep our connection, if we were going to survive this separation. The phone rang and rang and then rang once more.... When it was answered there were two voices that I heard on the receiving end. One voice was his roommate. The other voice was hers. Damn!

Tamekia Nicole

Why in the fuck was I so naïve? Why was I even surprised? I left and she came back. The roommate quickly said to her "it's not for you, hang up the phone." Everything around me became so quiet. I felt like I had suddenly became completely deaf.

I could barely hear the roommate repeatedly calling my name. But I felt the vibrations thru the phone and I snapped out of my shock. What you allow is what will continue. As soon as I was gone there she was. Loving him and becoming one with him. His roommate whispered into the phone. "He's in there with her," "I can go and call him to the phone if you want." I sat there on my bed dumbfounded and speechless. Now what in the fuck was I going to do? 24 hours later, I didn't even matter at least not to him. Finally, replying to his roommate "Don't bother calling him to the phone," "he's obviously busy." I hung up. I needed to get up. I had to conquer a whole new world. I could hear the pitter patter of my cousin's little feet just outside my bedroom door. That made me smile and took my mind off of him. The show must continue even if the band left.

Arizona was not off to a good start. This place already had me ready to flee. It was too hot. But I was going to tough it out and not run back to California. So I stopped calling. I stopped communicating and I stopped worrying. I did that well. I was beginning to enjoy church. I decided to give myself to the Lord. For a little while that eased the pain that I had. I was training myself to walk by faith and not by sight. The bible had more answers that I had ever fathomed, but probably because I never felt a pain like this. Adjusting to a lifestyle of church and family was easy. I was able to fully transition that into my everyday life. Every time I picked up my bible I was able to find the answers I needed. Lord knows I needed that. Everything that I ever worried about became obsolete.

I landed a wonderful job with American Express as a Credit Analyst. I worked from 5am to 2pm. All the free time I had, was spent at church. With my family or working out. I had exonerated all ill feelings towards my lover. I chose to concentrate on the most important element of my life…ME. Time came and time went. It had been an entire month with no contact with my lover. I was still breathing, still living and still functioning. I wanted and needed to hear his voice. I wanted to know what he was doing. But more importantly I wanted to know who he was doing it with. Love was making me do it. Love was still the master mind behind my steps. I should have already known by then that it wasn't love.

Tamekia Nicole

When I dialed his number, I listened intensely to every ring. Waiting for him to pick up…. he didn't, but his roommate did.

Thank God for nosey, back stabbing roommates. The roommate told me everything that I needed to hear. He also told me a lot of other things that I didn't want to hear. I listened to the cautionary advice that the roommate gave me. I set a plan in motion, to fly home to California. Honestly, how many times did I need to catch him in the act? How many times did I need to confront him? I had thoughts of killing him and her. Along with thoughts, of killing myself. At that point, I wish that I could have shaken some sense into myself.

The first piece of advice was "Make sure if you come for a visit you stay here at the house," "Don't let him talk you into staying the weekend in some hotel room" The second piece of advice was "You're too good to go thru this, with someone so undeserving." I paused for a moment. While the roommate was still talking, I was searching the internet for plane tickets. I found one for $500. So while the roommate was going blah, blah, blah in my ear. I was putting a $500 plan in motion. I was about stir some shit up. As soon I hung up, I started to cry. I started to be mad all over again. But instead of punching anything, I picked up my bible and read from Psalms. That soothed the storm that was brewing inside of me. That eased my desire of wanting to take my own life. I read until tears streamed down my face. I cried out for God to help me.

The next morning I called my lover. I told him I would be there the last week in November. Just like the roommate said, he insisted that we get some fancy hotel room. "No, I want to stay at the house. "That's where I feel comfortable." He paused and said "Ok." He showered me with meaningless I love you's and even kissed me thru the phone. My heart skipped a million beats. But I couldn't smile because I was planning a wicked weekend visit. Someone was going to get hurt. Hopefully, it wouldn't be me. After it's all said and done, there are a lot of things that could have been done different. I could have handled different. But I cannot say with confidence, that the end result would have been different. I honestly believe that my brain processes situations different, when matters of the heart are involved. When I don't process those matters accordingly, that's where my troubles begin.

Tamekia Nicole

Arizona wasn't a mistake. But I knew as frantic as I was on a constant basis. I needed to return to California. In between psychotic meltdowns and waiting for the day of my trip. I went to work and I went to church, to occupy my mind. *Operation make my lover see things my way,* was under way. I tossed and turned every night. I dreamt of him or them every night. I think I was going crazy. I was scared. I no longer owned or operated my own emotions.

How could I allow someone so far away be my puppet master? There was only one answer to that question...*Love Made Me Do It*. We had begun more consistent phone calls, as the date for my return inched closer. We even had phone sex one night. All I could think about was the real thing. That was too much power for one man to have I day dreamed about making love with Mary J Blige playing in the background. Now I'm sitting here miles away with a house full of kids and bibles. My lust for him was happening, and it was happening right now.

Don't get me wrong I wasn't dying to be noticed. I was noticed everywhere I went, even when I didn't want to be. There was a man that pursued me, a very nice guy from an affluent family...was the report I was given. A God fearing man, that went to the same church as I did. My family insisted I date him. *Please is all I said. My heart beats for one man and one man only.* That was the end of that conversation. Finally, it was the day to get on the plane for my weekend back to California. I felt like nothing in my closet looked good enough for him. None of my perfumes smelled good enough for him. My hair and nail same story. Everything was off, but my libido was ablaze. I was ready to be taken in his arms. I was ready for him to invade my insides. I wanted to feed him my soul and in return I would devour his.

Tamekia Nicole

CHAPTER 6

GOING BACK TO CALI

Tamekia Nicole

My lover was already at the airport when I arrived.   He was smiling and so was I. He was my knight and I was his damsel. However this damsel wasn't in distress she was horny. I hopped in the front seat of his truck, grabbed his free hand, placing it on my thigh.   I looked at him, nothing else mattered. The smile that he gave back to me was priceless.

There were a lot of perfect moments in the middle of all the dysfunction. Those few moments, kept me warm when our relationship grew cold. It's necessary to carry a few good memories of people even if they hurt you. After, he picked me up from the airport. We didn't go straight to his house. We rode around forever. He was wasting time. But I had been warned that, this is what he would do.   I tried not to panic. But in the back of my head I thought about what his roommate said. He implied that she was living there with my lover. After about 2 hours of doing nothing. We finally pull up to his house. Much to my dismay, I see her clothes piled up on the floor. There had to be a hidden camera somewhere. Recording these bullshit episodes of my life.

The bed was disheveled and the house was a mess. I was crushed to say the least. But instead of going off right then, I kicked her name brand shit under the bed. We sat in the living room. The living room where it all began and we just stared at each other.   Our vibe was definitely off. But hopefully that would change. I went over and sat on his lap. Held his face in my hands and kissed his lips. I knew this trip was about to go downhill. So I better make it count. We kissed and it felt damn good. My heart was warm, my panties were moist. This is what I came for. I came home to feel like I belonged to something and someone. I wanted to feel like I had a purpose.

I straddled him and I began undressing him.   But I would not allow him to carry me to that bedroom. He would have to take me where I was. The bedroom was their sanctuary. I wasn't ready to go in there just yet. He took his time, reacquainting his self with my erogenous zones. . It felt like we made love on the couch for hours. We were drenched in sweat and engulfed in a false reality. This was a perfect Friday night. But I was a bomb and I was ticking. Saturday, we left the house before noon. We went out visiting. Our vibe was still a little bit off. But we were warming up to each other. Once we put drugs into our system, our vibe would be perfect. When Saturday night came, he rolled up a few laced blunts.   We got high and I started to feel the devil brewing in my soul. He told me to

Tamekia Nicole

hold in the smoke, until I felt like my lungs couldn't take it. As long as the drugs kept coming and I felt bits and pieces of love, I didn't care if my lungs collapsed. Yes, it was that serious. We sat together in his room. My high eyes darted. I took mental inventory of things I seen of hers. I kept thinking in my head "Oh she lives here now." He said he had to step out. Perfect timing. I said "Ok." He doubled back "Johnson, don't touch shit."

CHAPTER 7

OH... SHE LIVES HERE NOW?

Tamekia Nicole

When the coast was clear, I took out her clothes from under the bed. I looked them over. I wasn't impressed. Fuck her and her clothes. I spit on those clothes and threw them back under the bed. I figured that wasn't enough though. I needed to really make her eat shit. He needed to eat shit too. But right now it was her turn. I would make sure that he had his turn very soon. On to the medicine cabinet. I know women she probably had high priced cosmetics and toiletries in there. Sure enough she did. When I was done she had containers filled with water and a toothbrush covered in shit. I heard him pull up I tried not to look suspicious. You can't play with the words... "I love you." It's not okay and he would find that out.

Drugs were like kryptonite to our already weak foundation. This was only the beginning. I felt slightly guilty. Not very guilty just a little bit. I just cleaned a toilet with her toothbrush. But I could find every reason why I did it and why it was okay. Was it really her fault that she was living with him? Or was he to blame or were they both at fault? I feel as if she broke the girl code. I also feel like he had no code. Anything went as long as it satisfied him. He was a consistent liar. Leaving me confused. Therefore we all maintained our spot, which was a constant state of deception, and betrayal. Was this part of the game? If so I needed to bow out gracefully. But I never had the courage to leave a situation where, I was an implied loser. If I left this situation I needed to feel like I was in complete control. Right now I was in control.

I sat there with a smirk on my face, on the edge of his bed in my boy shorts and my bra. I probably looked like I swallowed a canary. He came over to me and began to kiss my neck. I crisscrossed my legs behind his back and made him fall on top of me. He began tracing my skin, right along my hair line. He looked into my eyes "You know you're crazy right?" I smiled and said "Only in matters of my heart, so don't play, and don't hurt me," "Just love me the way that I love you." He moved off of me, like I struck a nerve. He needed to be real with me, but he wasn't. Instead, he told me that he went and picked up some pills. They would help us forget everything. We were already smoking blunts that were laced with cocaine. I was scared of what type of mood enhancement these drugs would cause. Would the interaction kill us?

My lover felt my concern even though I didn't say a word. "I'm not going to let anything happen to you." I said "ok" I popped my pill and

Tamekia Nicole

went to take a shower. When I was in the shower I felt the drugs hit my body like a ton of bricks. I felt good. Fresh out of the shower and sprawled out on the bed. He slathered baby oil all over me.

Oh my goodness his touch was everything. We talked, kissed, and fondled. Then he excused his self to roll a blunt, that he would be snow coating with cocaine. For reasons unknown to me at that time. My lover never ever allowed me to see him roll these blunts. He would just come with them already rolled. He had the blunt in hand and dived onto the bed. We made love. It was intense and surreal. It was illuminating and magical. All you could smell is sex and drugs. We were in a fog that was so dense you could cut thru it with a knife. The drug combination acted like a truth serum and he began telling me how much he missed me. He questioned when would return to California. I lowered my head "When I get better and you get rid of her." I knew I wasn't emotionally well. He knew that too. But he was a man and he was selfish. He wanted all of me when he wanted it. Not just when I wanted to give it. I probably reached at least eight climaxes that night.

Sunday, came so fast and today was the day I would get on a plane back to Arizona. Back to the suffocating heat. Back to being away from the reason I breathe…..him. I woke up naked and smiling and decided to cook breakfast. I felt my sense of being normal, seeping out of my body. I needed to act fast. Breakfast was a hit, we talked, laughed and channel surfed the morning away. I packed my stuff and then I decided to let it all out. "So she lives here now?" My lover stuttered, "Nah, she doesn't live here." "You're a muthafuckin' lie." "Why is all of her shit here?" My temperature and my voice began to rise. "You don't love me, you say it but you don't act like it." He said "Johnson, it's time to go to the airport".

I wasn't going anywhere and it would take hell and high water to make me go. He began putting my stuff in the truck. I didn't give a fuck at that point. He was going to listen to me. So I stood there and shook my head like a stubborn two year old. That's when shit got real. He picked me up and tried to physically move me out the front door. I held onto the pane of the doorway with all my might. I lost my grip. Now I was being carried and thrown into his truck. The ride to the airplane was brutal, no words, no tears and loud music. When I attempted to lower the volume, he grabbed my wrist. "You better be cool." I cried hysterically, "Why, why, why!" The airport was rapidly approaching. Pulling up to the curb at the airport. He jumped out and grabbed my luggage. I sat and watched. He tried to take me out the car. I held on tight "Please I love you, I don't wanna go." "I wanna stay with you, we love each other," one mad tear streaked down his cheek. "Get out." I sat at the airport hoping he would come back, he didn't. I boarded my plane. The tears on my face had dried up. I smiled thinking, that when they make love somebody would feel the panties that I left behind. That would let her know...I had been here. And I would be back. Sitting at the airport feeling stupid, but kind of satisfied at the same time. You want to feel important but you have to reserve your dignity. I left my dignity the same place I left my panties... in his bed.

Way before Beyoncé was singing about "Dangerous Love" I was living and breathing it. I didn't allow myself to think about what happened on my weekend trip, on my plane ride home. Thinking about him, her and us made my head ache. So I shut down all thoughts and just looked out the window. When I finally made it into the house I was exhausted. I had work at 5am so I crashed. I didn't dream. I didn't think. I just slept. When my alarm clock went off at 4am, I felt a sudden waive of sadness. I was once again alone. I wished I had one of those blunts to roll so that I could escape the inevitable. But I was out of my element I wouldn't even know, where to buy drugs at out here. I didn't need drugs anyway. That would just cause a whole other set of problems. So as I slowly peeled myself out of bed. I had to do what was necessary, for me to survive. I kneeled down and prayed. I asked God, to remove everyone from my life that meant me harm.

Through all my self-inflicted mayhem, God has never let me down. Prayer worked for months to come. Christmas came and went and I had no contact with my lover. Whenever my phone rang, it was only people I didn't want to talk to.

CHAPTER 8

A BRAND NEW YEAR

Tamekia Nicole

New Year's come and went. I carried on with my life as best as I could. Until, I couldn't take it anymore. His birthday was coming up. That would be my segway back into his life. But I couldn't swallow my pride to call on the exact day. So I called the weekend after. The roommate answered and boy did he have a lot to tell me. The roommate was evidence that men tend to gossip more than women. Especially, if they think that they're going to get some pussy. I listened intently as he told me about my lover and his girlfriend. I held my anger in. So that I could continue hearing the information if his roommate thought I was mad he would stop talking. These two were having the time of their life. Plus, my lover's two kids were visiting for the summer. *What a happy fucking family they must be.*

My heart sank with every word about their love. I almost hung up the phone. Until, I heard that my lover was leaving her with the kids every day and disappearing at night. I thought to myself... *ha ha, bitch, that's what you get.* A tiger never changes their stripes. Just like men, they are creatures of habit. Bound to do the same things, always. I wrapped up the conversation with the roommate. When I closed my eyes I saw a glimmer of hope...the glimmer of happily ever after. Maybe I was the one. Maybe I could change him in a way that she couldn't. He was my tiger. I called again the next day and my lover answered the phone. I wished him a happy belated birthday and told him that I loved him dearly. He remained silent.

It was a hard transition for both of us and I felt that thru the awkward silence. He broke his silence with an "I love you too Petunia." I loved that pet name. That solidified our union, at least for that moment. But things were different. A lot of time had lapsed. I had done a lot of praying when we weren't talking. I was hoping that my obedience to God would change our relationship. God showed me things that I wasn't able to recognize before. I had a vision of what I wanted my relationship to look like with the man in my life. As hard as I prayed, I felt like that call could be the start of a new beginning. But there was still her.

God made me a lover and I never denied that calling. I am thankful for that blessing. I say that to say this. I understood why she didn't let go. I understood why and how she loved my lover. I could hate her, which I did. But I also understood her. I wondered if we could all just live together and please him. Cohabitate in peace and love, but that

Tamekia Nicole

was never going to happen. So I let go for that moment after the phone call ended. I wished him the best in life and love.

As I continued to live and I reflect on what God needed and wanted me to be. I made wonderful friends and prayer warriors at my church. I gained a deeper understanding of the bible and I was even baptized. I had a renewed strength. As I found more strength to approach my life, I found a lack of balance in other places. It was always something.

Working at American Express was wonderful, church life was great, but there was a severe lack of structure in the household I was living in. Slowly, I was losing my patience and it was showing. I admit that I'm not the easiest person to get along, especially if I'm depressed. But without structure and balance, situations are guaranteed to arise. I had been in Arizona for 4 1/2 months. It was time for me to go back to California. My sister was enticing me to come back and live with her. Even though we were often like oil and vinegar. I gave it some thought. Then I had a call from my love. It was like he read my mind and felt my heart. Only soul mates have that connection. It had been almost two months since our last conversation. It was ironic that he called. I made up my mind. I was going home to California.

I had sent him a care package as a late birthday gift. It included a Men's Devotional Bible, his favorite cologne and a letter telling him where my heart was at. My heart would always be in tune with his even when we were apart. He was very thankful. "So when are you coming back?" "I'll be home next month." God was good and I was going to work on me. Hopefully, my lover could be included in this new journey of self-discovery and spirituality. If not, then I would probably have to fuck him up. I knew that no matter what happened. When I went back to California it was guaranteed, to be full of unexpected surprises. But I was ready. With God for me, who could be against me?

CHAPTER 9

GETTING BACK TO HIM

Tamekia Nicole

Honestly, I don't think that I was really ready to go back to California. Spiritually I felt that I was ready to go back. But I know myself. I was too anxious. Once again love was making me do it. Love was driving every muscle in my body and controlling my thoughts. Even if things didn't go how I wanted them to go. I needed to see the downward spiral first hand. Sounds crazy right? I think so too.

I know that being molested plays a huge role in my life and my intimate interactions with men. I was uprooting myself again, for reasons that made no sense. I lacked rational judgment when it came to my lover. Once a love like that starts to possess you, it becomes an addiction. You will do anything to experience that high. The move from Arizona was a smooth transaction, for the most part. I quit my good job. Said good bye to the few friends I had and began to plan my life back home. Just as we discussed I went to live with my sister, her fiancé and my nephew. When I came home it felt foreign to me. As soon as I was settled, I called him. He answered but then gave the phone to his roommate. Something I shouldn't have tolerated. The roommate told me that he would call me back. But he didn't call back.

Instead, they showed up at my sister's house. When I heard the knock at the door I had a feeling that it was him. We were connected like that. As soon as I opened up the door he hugged me like only he could. It was such a wonderful, warm and loving. There we were in the door way of my sister's apartment. Back in each other's arms. Life was as good as it could get. I let him and the roommate in the house. We all sat in the living room. I went and sat on my lovers lap and held is face in my hands. He smiled. He asked if we could talk outside. "Of course we can." What he told me caught me off guard. I had to ask for his roommate when I called. If it was cool, he would get on the phone. But if it wasn't cool that he would have to call me back. I knew it. Nothing had change. Moving back would have to be about me and my life. If I left it solely in his hands, I would be hurt...and he would be dead.

I didn't even know how to process what he said to me. I stayed silent. We went back in the house. I sat there stunned and dizzy, fighting back my tears. The next few days were a blur. I couldn't I sleep, or eat. I could barely talk. I literally walked around like a mute. Luckily my sister didn't play...grown people don't get to mope around the house. So after a week of moping, I got off the couch and started looking for a job. I won't

Tamekia Nicole

lie I followed his directions on how to call him. But that only led to arguments. Eventually she caught on, that I was back in town. I knew that technically I was in the wrong. I was breaking the girl code. He had a woman. They were in an active relationship. But I wanted him back and he was mine. Period. Point. Blank. It was obvious that my lover and I were going to fade out of each other lives. I just didn't know when. Every time I heard her voice and she heard mine, it was never good. The words that we exchanged were extreme low blows. One night our arguing was so volatile. I begged my sister for her car keys. So that I could drive over there and fight her, my sister wasn't having it. Eventually, my lover blocked my phone number from being able to call his house. I found my way around that. I was crafty, impulsive, and obsessed. I called one night but to my dismay they weren't home. Instead I had a lengthy conversation with the roommate. This was a prelude to another set of problems that I would acquire.

I was naïve, and depressed. Eventually, the roommate and I started to have an affair. Not a sexual affair. But an affair of like-minded brains and hearts. We bother were attempting to achieve a common ground. Love. But looking back, he was trying to acquire pussy and have one up on my lover. At first it was totally innocent, but it was emotionally orgasmic. I was getting information about my loves relationship. Being heard and being able to vent. But in between I was being flirted with. We emailed each other poetry and witty statements. I was falling in love with his mind. Honestly I never gave a fuck about the roommate. Only what he could do for me.

I wanted to make love to my man and live happily ever after. But every time I was in close proximity to him. I started to feel disgusted. I didn't want him to touch me and then go crawl in the bed with her. I didn't want to smell her perfume. It was too much. I wanted to kill myself and bypass all the bullshit. My lover finally realized that it was over, when we went to the Oakland Zoo on a date. We sat in the car and began kissing. It felt weird. He felt weird. The ridges in his muscles felt foreign. His smell was unfamiliar to me. Everything was off balance. None the less, he moved his seat back from the steering wheel. I hopped on top of him. We bumped and grinded. He tugged at my zipper and I moved his hand. Then I backed up and got off of him. As horny as I was I didn't want him to touch me. I wanted a man's touch. He wasn't a man, he was a cheater. As he tried to get in my

Tamekia Nicole

pants, I had racing thoughts of them in the bed. Instantly, my libido and eagerness went limp. As if I had a dick. He backed up and started the engine. *Oh well. Take me home.* No eye contact or conversation as we drove to my house. I jumped out the truck and he took off. I was trying to reach out to him. He was giving me nothing to work with. I would give back even less than that.

CHAPTER 10

THE ROOMMATE

Love Made Me Do It

Tamekia Nicole

I was fed attention and energy from the roommate. Even though, I knew that this could be a potentially disastrous situation. But I needed to stir the pot a little bit. In the mean time I looked for a job. So that I didn't stay at my sister's house, longer than necessary. Since I just left American Express., I had no problem finding a job that was equally as good. I started working at a Marble and Granite Company. About three weeks after I returned back to California. Me and my lover were hit and miss. There was no intimate interaction between us. But there was plenty intellectual stimulation going on with his roommate. It was hard to imagine myself with someone other than my love. But it was obvious that he felt another way.

Our relationship should have been a slam dunk. But my lover made it hard. While I was transitioning myself back to California living and figuring out my love life. I made a friend at my new job that still plays a monumental role in my life. Living with my sister just like when, you live with anybody started to get old. She was very particular as to how she liked her house to be run. But honestly a one bedroom was too small for all of us. Then, just as I knew it would… shit hit the fan. My belongings were packed up and placed on the porch.

There was no blame in the situation. Just not enough room, for more than one alpha personality. I had a job, and I had money. But now I needed a place to live ASAP. I stayed in a hotel room for about one week, while I searched for an apartment or roommate situation. I found a condo, and the location was perfect. I was moving directly across the street from them both. Even though I asked the roommate how he felt about me living across the street from them. I was going to do what I wanted to do. Luckily, for me he was passive aggressive and in love with me. He didn't care. So I moved in.

As the roommate and I were getting closer, I urged him to tell my love what was going on. I felt kind of like it was the right thing to do or maybe I just wanted to be mean. You can't hurt me and just think that's okay. The roommate was nice. But I knew that sooner or later. He would want more of me, than I had given at that point. As soon as he told my lover about our interactions, I received a call. "You ain't shit." I laughed so hard my eyes watered. I hug the phone up. My lover didn't even know that he just cussed out his new neighbor! The situation was out of control and so was my life.

Love Made Me Do It

Tamekia Nicole

My new place was great. My roommate was awesome and I had a budding friendship with my coworker. My coworker had invited me out with her and her family and I couldn't wait to hang out. I need to take my mind off of my problems. She introduced me to her best friend, sisters, brothers, and cousins. As soon as her brother and cousin saw me they started messing with me. Wondering, who I was. I loved the attention. That night would be the first of many nights filled with fun. Their whole crew became my new addiction. The timing of meeting new friends didn't sit well with the roommate, who had graduated to being my boyfriend.

With my lover completely out of my life, things were better. But the roommate was so insecure. He didn't want to let me out of his sight. I owed him a little more respect than what I was giving him. Although we were in a relationship, he was fearful of my lover because of the decision he had made to be with me. I drove the roommate's car like it was mine. I let my friends drive it. I was spent his money like it was mine and I was eating dinner every Sunday with his parents. In order for me to reap these small rewards, I had to put up with unnecessary paranoia. He wanted me to drive an alternate route home so that my lover wouldn't see me. He wanted me to move when my lease was up. Plus he wanted to call me by my middle name.

During this time I thought to myself...he should know that I was vulnerable and weak for my lover and not for him. I wished he would stop acting like he didn't know that. But I played along. I fed his ego. I eventually fed his loins too. I kind of knew what I was doing, kind of. Did the roommate and I have sex...? Yes we did....Was it amazing? No, it was awkward. He was still living in the house with my lover and his girlfriend. I was living across the street, casing their every move. This was a hard job. I was constantly trying to position myself to be seen by my love. The first four months I was living there. I never saw him. But during those months I was being showered with gifts from the roommate. I gracefully accepted every gift. I was caught in a world wind of emotions, erratic thoughts. I was in a spider web of deceit and betrayal. This was hard.

What do you do when the person you love the most; more than yourself... is with someone else and you've decided to have an affair with his best-friend? No matter how I tell the story. It never sounds right. My lover and the roommate never fought about me. At least, not to my

Tamekia Nicole

knowledge. Boom, boom, boom…"Tamekia, open up this door!" I ran to the door. Unaware, of the bad news awaiting me on the other side.

It was the roommate. He told me that my lover and his girlfriend had been arguing like cats and dogs. Then he started going off about me. He ranted about us being together. Allegedly, my lover said "Johnson is mine blood, until I say other –wise." "But now you're putting your dick inside of her?" "What the fuck is wrong with you?" When this was told to me, initially I was in shock. But I felt that those were words of love, jealousy and envy. My lover was just mad because it wasn't him. This confirmed that I had his attention. But all attention isn't good attention. I wish I knew that then. My next move I made would have to be more hurtful than the move before.

CHAPTER 11

NEIGHBORS

Tamekia Nicole

What exactly was it that I was trying to accomplish? What is it that I needed from him? I burned through those questions so many times in my head I was tired of them. But I wouldn't stop making moves until those answers came to me. I was sick of the roommate already. He was so dramatic and unnerving that I couldn't think straight. He had the ability to give me everything I wanted. But I just didn't want it with him. But I played the part. I accepted his love but it was hard to reciprocate because I didn't feel the same. I did love him, but there was no spark. I wanted who I wanted. Only God could change that. The roommate knew...he had too, at least by now.

When he spoke of my lover I had a twinkle in my eye. When he talked about himself it had less of an effect on me. I was wrong. But I wasn't sure how to stop this monster that was driving me to be so mean, bitter and obsessive. So time went on and we continued *to be together and date*. We had adventures. We had an intellectual connection but I was starved for something that he couldn't feed me. My life was good if you just took a glance at it from the outside. I had a good job, made new friends, had an awesome roommate. But in between it all, there was a devil and an angel sitting on my shoulders. Unfortunately, I was always siding with the devil. My patience was running thin. I had yet to be seen by my lover. He had yet to see that I was living right across the street from him. I felt like a private eye, watching and waiting. Then more watching and waiting. My anxiety and blood pressure were through the roof. The roommate started storing things at my house because he was plotting to move out. So every night, I lay and stare at his belongings. Disgusted with myself.

Admittedly, I was being selfish. I never gave a fuck when he would moan and groan about my lover finding out that I lived across the street. "Get over it!" "He knows that we're fucking, and soon he will know that I live across the street." That was my only response to this same old, tired, ass discussion between us. We were both accountable for this fiasco. He just needed to ride this out. I was still the center of my own existence and therefore my happiness came first." I partied with my new friends'. I experienced Oakland and parted with San Jose. I drank *Bad Apples*. I was known for partying till the sun came up or until I threw up. I clubbed almost every night of the week and would slither in the house around 3am. Sleep for a few hours, and then go to work...

Tamekia Nicole

The solidarity that I experienced with my new friends was similar to that of a family. I desperately needed to feel like I belonged to something and someone. My club life started to make my boyfriend feel insecure. So I took the advice of my coworker. I started going off on him every time he opened his mouth to complain, about what I was doing. Sometimes I would just look at him with so much disgust. But sometimes his words were so heartfelt. Especially, when he told me how much he loved me. There were way too many conversations like that towards the end. That's when I knew that I would have to end this. Although, he was a man with good intentions towards I didn't want him.

So I kept the brick wall up. Only removing some bricks, when I felt the need to have sex. I refused to take my wall all the way down for him. More time passed and then the day came…. when I was seen. Four months later. I made my debut as my lover's neighbor! Nobody was ready for the scene that was about to be made. I remember the day like it was yesterday. I was going to the store with my roommate. As soon as I stepped foot off the porch I saw him. I was so scared I backed up. My roommate turned to me "Girl, come on…he's nobody." So I followed her lead to the car. He was in his backyard with his skinny bitch. Since he was so tall he saw me over the fence. I never saw my lover move so fast. He started coming towards me, but stopped in the middle of the street. She was tugging at the back of his shirt.

I stood tall, and with confidence. While he ranted and yelled at me from his side of the street, I just smiled. He was accusing me of breaking into his house. I smirked and shrugged. Whatever else he said, my heart beat, drowned it out. I was winning and my lover would soon be back where he belonged. With me. I got into my roommates car, let the seat back and smiled. I was content. I was ready to begin taking back what was mine. To be madly in love is a gift and a curse. I was madly in love. I was deep in love. The voice of reason was long gone.

CHAPTER 12

LOVE THY NEIGHBOR, LIKE YOU LOVE THYSELF

Tamekia Nicole

My every waking thought revolved around being with him. I was definitely a young woman with insecurity issues. I needed reassurance and nurturing. But I had no idea how or where to receive any of that. These problems were my own. But, I thought love could fix them. I was as transparent as I could be regarding my lover and his roommate. I don't know if that transparency hurt me or helped me. Sometimes too much transparency can hurt you. Only, because other people don't know how to respond to that…or they use it against you.

I slept like a baby that night. I dreamt about being with him and causing discord in his relationship. I woke up the next morning feeling like a million bucks. This was it, my big break. My relationship with the roommate was on a fast track downhill. I couldn't wait for it to be over and done with. But I knew that I would have to be the one to pull the trigger. I did just that. I was going to Chabot Jr College taking a night class and the roommate picked me up every night. This night was no different. Accept he had no idea about the bomb I was about to drop. I got in the car and I looked at him….. "I don't want to do this anymore," he looked at me and starting crying. "I knew you would do this, I knew you would break my heart." There was nothing I could say. "I'm sorry, can you just take me home."

That night my heart sank and I felt as if I reached an all-time low in my life. I hurt someone who probably really loved me. I lay in the bed looking at all his junk stored in my bedroom. I tried everything to get a good night's sleep. Right when I started to drift off, "Johnson, Johnson," then it was louder "TAMEKIA, TAMEKIA….I KNOW YOU HEAR ME…GET UP!"… It was the roommate he was in my backyard. I opened my window "Dude, what do you want… it's 3am?" "Get the fuck out of here?" "Give me my gun!" Shaking my head in disbelief I just replied "No!" I closed my blinds and my window and lay back down. When he had moved most of his stuff to my house to store, one of those items was a gun. There was no way in hell that I was giving him this gun.

The morning came and I looked out into my backyard and of course he wasn't there. But I had a million missed calls from this maniac. I checked my voicemail and he left a message saying that he left my lovers house and would not be going back there. He had stolen his company cell phone and if I needed to reach him that was the only way. Fuck! Seriously this is not the way I wanted to start my day! I had created a

Tamekia Nicole

monster. *Now love was making him do it.* I called him, and told him to come and get his gun and all the other shit he left behind. He pulled up to my house in his work truck. He didn't take any of his items accept the gun. I still had the keys to the mustang. I would be keeping those until I felt like giving them back.

I was on pins and needles wondering if I would see him on the news. It was like I had been holding my breath and I desperately needed to exhale. I needed to live. I needed to feel. I was praying, and wishing that ending it with the roommate, would allow me to rectify my life. Of course an escape is never easy. Breakups never just end in one day. He showed up at my house begging to talk to me for a few minutes, so I let him in. I sat on my bed expecting him to sit next to me so we could talk. Instead he got down on one knee and asked me if I would marry him.

What in the fuck is going on? I was continuously caught in a storm drain and garbage kept falling on me. I said no. I had to say no. I didn't love him. I didn't love him like he deserved. I think at that point I didn't even love myself. I wanted to be with my neighbor....my lover... I already had proved over and over again that I loved him. More than I loved anything else. I loved thy neighbor, just like I loved thyself. The bible says that is what you are supposed to do. See my mind set was always like that. Looking for justification for the bullshit I was doing.

Looking back now... I think that saying no to a person that had been so good to me, may have been one of my biggest regrets in life. But I would have dogged him in a marriage, much worse than I did in our relationship. This I knew for a fact. He left, only returning to get his car keys. This was wrong. He was hurt and he was picking up his Mustang on an empty tank. Plus a scratched bumper. It was a cold world I was living in. So if it was cold for me, I was going to make sure it was icy for everyone else. There is no fury like a woman scorned.

CHAPTER 13

JUGGLING ACTS

Tamekia Nicole

The days rolled by and my life continued. I had met yet another man. I really hoped that he would take me away from my thoughts and worries. He was my best friend's cousin. He was fun, handsome, hood, and charming. It was nothing serious though...we drank, we smoked, and we chilled. We had amazing sex and he made me laugh. I thought those were perfect qualities for me. I loved seeing my new friend lying next to me after a Friday night of drinking. But I would soon be put in a position to choose between fun and love. I was hung over and I needed to get up to let my handsome guest out. We kissed and I told him I would page him later. 5 minutes later I heard a knock at my front door. I ran to get it thinking it was my handsome overnight guest and he forgot something. The knocking persisted so I yelled out; "Who is it?" The reply I got almost knocked me off my feet.

"It's your neighbor, and I wanted to know if you had a cup of sugar I could borrow?" I peered out the blinds and it was him...it was my lover! I opened the door. He grabbed me and hugged me, pulled back, looked at me and kissed me. This is what I wanted my life to be about. Him. When we finally pulled back from kissing... I said "I'm sorry neighbor, we ran out of sugar. My hearts delight and my reason for breathing had found his way across the street to kiss me. Everything I desired had been granted in that moment. We sat on the couch across from one another and it all came back to me. All the love. Even all the disappointment but those thoughts disappeared when he pulled out the drugs. Then I was filled with anxiety. As I watched the man I love get ready to intoxicate me, with something I soon wouldn't be able to live without. Cocaine.

Sitting in my living room looking at my lover was an amazing feeling. I could barely keep it together, my legs were shaking and my voice was quivering when I spoke. We sat there for all of 2 minutes and then he asked to go to the bathroom so that he could roll one up. My anxiety level was at its peak while I waited for him to roll this. He had this devilish smirk on his face when he came out the bathroom...he said "Where we blowin this at?" I had no idea. I knew that I shouldn't smoke anything in the house. But oh well. I was about to put one in the air with the love of my life. I grabbed his hand, and I lead him up the stairs.

I grabbed a towel and stuffed in the gap under my bedroom door. He fired up the blunt. "Remember when you hit this, you hold in the

Tamekia Nicole

smoke until you can't anymore....then blow it out slowly." I did just as I was told. I scooted closer to him.

We smoked and smoked, everything began to get a little hazy. We started getting horny. Leaning in simultaneously. We combined our lips. Our tongues danced. He lay down and I straddled him. He griped my hips like he owned them. This was what it was about....the passion, the fire, being joined together on a level that no one could ever understand. But then real life kicked back in.

My high was coming down and I quickly came back to reality. Sure I loved him. But now what? Instead of questioning him, I told him I had shit to do and needed to get dressed. I got up and walked him to the door. I kissed him goodbye and he said "I love you Johnson." "I know and I love you too." After I closed the door I watched him from the window as he walked back across the street. There went my baby. I was strutting around the house like I had just won the Lotto. You couldn't tell me shit. Life went on as I was used to it. Working and partying. But then work took an unexpected twist. Calls on top of calls; on top of more calls, at work. I got a call from the skinny bitch. This made me want to choke the life out of her. "Good afternoon this is Tamekia," there was silence "You fuckin my man?" I said "Not yet, and last I checked he was mine and will continue to be. "It's not where he's at its where he wants to be." She hung up. I wasn't willing to call her back from my job. I wasn't risking my bread and butter for her or him.

On my drive home I was thinking of clever and insulting things to say to her. I couldn't wait to call that whore back and tell her a few things. I picked up my phone dialed the number and low and behold I was blocked...again. I sat there in disbelief. I ran over to the window and looked over across the street. I could see two silhouettes, his & hers. I wish I was a fly on that wall. I could only hope that he was telling that bitch to get out. I was definitely a dreamer. I was drawn to my lover like a moth to a flame.... literally. The mere thought of him made my knees weak, and my temperature rise. Between the love, the imbalance, the lust and the drugs we were sure to be the death of each other.

Tamekia Nicole

Anything that needed to be done I was going to do it. ESPECIALLY, if it brought us closer together. I was willing to lie, cheat, steal, and put my life on the line for him. Till death or drugs do us part. Waiting for the perfect moment is always hard. When you're in love there is no such moment. When I think about all the reasons I kept running the race towards my lover. The only thing I can think of is. I didn't want anyone else to have the happiness that I felt he could give me.

No matter how damaged or how imperfect he was. I was unconditionally in love with every ounce of him. Day after day I watched him. I know that he watched me too. From the mailbox to my car. From his car to his front door. We were a pair of eyes watching and waiting for moments that we could be with each other. I lived for all those moments. I loved feeling him inside me. I loved waiting and wondering when and if he would call. I loved HIM and I couldn't wait for the day that we would be ONE. No sneaking and no hiding. I had the feeling that him and the skinny bitch would be coming to an end. Being the patient woman that I was. I had all the time in the world. I enjoyed watching the house they built become unraveled. We spoke a lot while we were at work. We were transitioning back into each other's life and I loved the experience.

The skinny bitch wore herself out calling me at work. I finally broke down and told the bitch to call me at home. Eventually the phone calls died down. The only thing now was me and him. She moved out. Every second of every day I could only think about him. On Friday nights it was me and him. I would watch him pull out everything he needed to roll the magic blunts. He needed scissors to cut the blunt open, a cutting board to section off and cut the weed, a razor blade to break down the coke and a lighter to dry the masterpiece. We smoked that Friday night, blunt after blunt after blunt. When the last one was rolled and smoked. He looked in his wallet and I looked in mine. Between us there was $100 towards our party. We connected, we talked. Our souls connected like it was the very first time. We fell in love all over again. Those drugs were powerful, the smoke alone grabbed ahold of your senses. Making sure you didn't have the capacity to have a rational, logical thought. Drugs and Love were, the only thing on the menu.

Love Made Me Do It

Tamekia Nicole

My afternoon was lazy that Saturday and my body was worn out. There were no thoughts in my head. But... how good I felt and how could I bottle that emotion. My phone rang interrupting my thoughts and it was him. "Hello?" ..."Johnson is that you?"....."Yes baby it's me..." "I love you..."and "I love you too...." This shit don't stop. It couldn't stop I would beg and pray for years that it wouldn't stop. Had I known then what I know now. I should have quit then.

But the sex was good, the memories were priceless and those drugs were everything. I needed all that shit to function at a level that kept me smiling. We were young, reckless, lust filled; with not one care in the world. We were on the path of living fast and dying young. This was fine with me. As long as we were together. The skinny bitch left behind pieces of her existence in the. I really didn't care. I also had life outside of my lover. I was still fucking my best friend's cousin. The TOWN night life was nothing like what I had experienced in San Jose. The amount of fun I was being exposed to should have been illegal. I think a lot of it was, but it was fun. It kept me occupied. I was juggling work, school, friends, family and two men.

If I allowed my mind to get idle at any point. I would start to concoct crazy ideas and there was no point in being unnecessarily crazy. I could use that when I really needed to act up. So between work, partying, dating my best friends cousin AND my lover I was really busy. This was good. My roommate was hardly ever home. When she was, she was either in the kitchen or with her legs to her headboard. Life was good. It had simplified a tiny bit. The skinny bitch was out of sight and out of mind. My best friends cousin was everything...he rocked my world, and made me smile. My lover was on speed dial. My mind was occupied and my soul was fed. I paid a heavy price down the line, to have false peace of mind. On more than one occasion, the cousin had just dropped me off and my lover was stalking my moves. Calling me as soon as my foot hit the porch. "Hello". "And, who was that nigga droppin you off?" I loved it.

I loved the interrogation and the attempt at being jealous. Those moments were sexy. I would never respond to those sarcastic remarks and questions. I would simply say... "Do you want me to come over or not?" Like I said, life was good.

Tamekia Nicole

I was being greedy and I felt that I had earned a little greed. Only when it was too late, did I realize that I was robbing myself of self-decency. I stifled my own growth. I needed to get to know myself, and what was healthy for me to seek from the men in my life. The cousin wasn't at all bad for me. He was a welcomed humorous edition to my life and to my bed. But eventually I started to be flakey with him. I started spending more time with my lover. My heart couldn't manage the juggling act. Other people noticed it and so did the cousin…

The cousin and I were cooling off and we didn't even return each other's calls or pages until days later. That was real life. You didn't get closure. You just separated and dealt with it. I dropped all my balls, no more juggling.

CHAPTER 14

LIFE WAS GOOD

Love Made Me Do It

Tamekia Nicole

Life was STILL good. Me and my lover were like conjoined twins. My birthday was wonderful I spent it with my friends and partied the night away. My weekends were filled with him and cocaine. The drugs snowed us in every weekend. Or every time we had money to blow. There were no limits on how we expressed our love. The cocaine enhanced every emotion. My tolerance for the laced blunts had increased as did his. So more money was spent too achieve our first high. I still didn't recognize that he had a problem, and that I was right behind him. Love, sex and drugs go good together and whoever said it doesn't... is lying.

Eventually, my roommate asked to talk to me about living there. We decided that since I am never there. It didn't make any sense to pay rent in a place that I never sleep at. So there it was. I didn't want to say anything to my lover right away. We were getting along perfectly. I must have been really in tune with God because all of my prayers were answered in reference to my love affair. Christmas came and went I spent it with my mom, and my granny nothing fancy. The New Year was upon us and I was spending it with my lover. I was so nervous it was crazy trying to get ready. All my clothes looked wrong; hair wasn't actin right, no matching bra & panties! But finally I pulled it together.

We decided that we would get dressed up and just chill at the house. That was perfect. We sat on the leather sectional; drinking champagne, kissing in between sips, and smoking cocaine & weed. I can't really remember what we talked about. But I know that it was the first time since we had reconnected. That I felt like we were emotionally on the same page at the same time. Those feelings are the ones that lovers live for...the connecting of souls. That is what we always had. We talked that night until the sun came up. Bringing in the New Year together and then he asked me to move in. I couldn't believe it. A kiss sealed the deal.

I went to bed feeling high and wonderful. But I woke up groggy, head pounding with the driest mouth. I looked around he was right next to me sound asleep. I loved him, he meant everything to me. Everything about him, in my eyes was perfect. I laid back down snuggling right against his back. The warmth of his skin and the rhythm of his heart beat lulled me back to sleep. He made me feel safe.

Tamekia Nicole

When we woke up on that 1st day of the New Year is was nighttime. Drugs & champagne were behind our 12 hour hibernation. I had a new lease on life. Yup, life was GOOD. I couldn't wait to move in. It was Monday and I was set to move in on that Friday. All week I had so much anxiety. Friday finally came! I packed my last box and I was ready to walk everything over. I had already loaded up my car and parked it on the opposite side of the street. I was going to be closing that front door for the last time. What a good feeling.

5pm, and I was sitting waiting on the porch for him to come home. I didn't even have the key to the house yet. At 6pm and I was still sitting in that same spot watching all the cars come and go. Trying to determine if the headlights I seen were his. Finally, around 7pm he pulled up. I had such an attitude. I felt like maybe he forgot today was the first day of the rest of our life. He didn't forget, he just didn't care and this was a constant pattern with him. But because I was so love sick and insecure it often didn't matter what he did or how he did it. He stepped out of the truck happy, but when he saw my sour face... that happy expression dissipated. I tried to clean up my attitude and my body language. But I just couldn't get it together. I asked him for the key and he gave it to me.

Then he said he would be back, he was going out. So there I sat. There would be many nights just like that, he went out...and I stayed home. After a while we started to get in rhythm with each other and we started having a really good time. Some of my clothes were in the spare bedroom and some were in the bedroom that we shared. It was like we were together but separate. Work was a drag. My best friend no longer worked there. It impossible for me to fuck with the women in my office. I couldn't be fake or phony. Not even for the sake of work. I looked forward to the end of the day with him and the drugs. On most days he would already have a chopper rolled filled with weed and cocaine.

He had given me a new nickname "The 4:45 lady" because that was the exact time I came home every day, with an attitude. But his face and that blunt always made the 4:45 lady disappear. That was the benefit of drugs and love. They were so good they made you forget your problems even the ones you had 2 minutes ago. I would hurry and take a shower and lotion up and sit in my panties, so we could smoke. That smoke was good to me. It was good to us, it elevated our love making. But

Tamekia Nicole

while we were making love, in the back of my head I would be hoping that another blunt would follow that one. That was the addict in me growing.

CHAPTER 15

DRUGS & LOVE

Tamekia Nicole

We started to not get along because the money was going too fast. I was working and bringing in decent money. He was laid off and collecting a nice chunk from the unemployment department. But 2-300 dollar every other day was getting to be a bit much for drug money. I noticed that bills weren't being paid. However, there was always a bountiful supply of narcotics and weed. Something wasn't right but I didn't have the courage to say anything. I just kept doing what I supposed to do. This was going to work and put in my share.

My party life with my friends had taken a nose dive since I couldn't see past him. Even when he went out. I just wanted to stay home and wait for him to get back. My friends were irritated with me but I could care less. I had started getting thin because of the drugs. So I stopped coming around as much. My whole life revolved around ways to make him happy and using drugs. His mom would often come over and visit with us they were really close. She was at the house one day and I overheard her ask him…Why did he need so much money to pay bills? She had just given him several hundred dollars. I listened real close, I was curious as to how he would answer. I was working putting in my share, he was getting a check and supposedly putting in his share too AND he was getting money from his mom.

This didn't sound right and it definitely was not adding up. As he would do for years to come, he told lies to cover up the truth. I decided that eavesdropping on their conversation was not my immediate concern. As long as there was no disconnect notices or eviction letters. I was going to hope and pray that this man….my man…. was taking care of business. Drugs and more drugs. We spent absurd amounts of money on drugs. If you looked in our refrigerator there wasn't shit in it but eggs, gas station burritos, hot sauce and maybe some Tampico juice. There was no money to do fun things like go eat, or go to the movies. There was barely enough money for gas. We forsake having gas in both cars for having bigger supply of drugs. His mom started noticing little differences in both of us, but mainly her son. She loved going to the movies and wanted us to go with her one day. But we didn't have enough money to go. That was no problem for her his mom was very generous. She liked me, I worked, I chipped in, and I kept the house clean, and cooked when there was food. Most importantly, I loved her son.

Love Made Me Do It

Tamekia Nicole

I felt like me and my lover, were becoming a little family. We were all going to see Spider Man. I was excited but something wasn't right. My lover had been acting weird. I felt as if it was another woman and it probably was. To keep it real. I was trying to train a dog. He wasn't a puppy, he was set in his ways. One woman could never satisfy every desire that he had. We argued that day like we never argued before. We were supposed to be getting ready for the movies. When I brought up his attitude and how he had been treating me. He brought up the roommate and how I fucked the roommate. "You've have fucked so many girls, who gives a fuck if I fucked him," "Get over it."

He didn't like that answer but it was the truth. I felt like if that was still going to be a topic...that could cause a heated discussion. Then we shouldn't be living together. This argument had us going back and forth from room to room. Yelling and cussing. We were detoxing from drugs. It had been a few days. Money was low plus we were going to be with mama all day. We couldn't get high. I followed him into the bedroom, because I was still trying to get my point across. That's when he slapped me. That was the very first time he physically laid a hand on me. He grabbed my arm and told me to shut the fuck up. I could say was "Please, don't hit me again." But instead, he closed the door on my bare foot. He didn't care about the pain in my foot or my shattered dignity. Definitely not my self-worth. He cared more about what would his mama would think if we looked like we had been fighting. So I dried my tears and put on a happy face. I never forgot the physical pain. I felt worthless. I thought to myself...*I'm paying more than half the bills, tolerating hoe behavior from him, supplying us with endless hundred dollar bills to feed our addiction and you put your hands on me.*

Too bad I never said anything that day. I may have been able to save myself from the many ass whoopins down the line. Saying something that very first day instead of cowering and crying could have changed a million things in my world. But I didn't say anything. My lips only let out small sobs. I ranted and talked loud but my bark was much louder than my bite.

CHAPTER 16

TO MUCH TIME ON OUR HANDS

Tamekia Nicole

On top of our volatile relationship, I started having more problems at work then I could handle. I knew I needed to get it together. It was hard. I was emotionally distressed and it showed. Yeah life wasn't that good anymore. Life sucked. My friends or being around them didn't interest me. Nothing was fun. I was agitated and sleepy all the time. There would be some days when I would walk across the street and visit with my old roommate. Even she noticed that I had become increasingly slim. I brushed off her inquiry when she asked if I was okay. It really wasn't her business. Plus, I didn't give a fuck about what she had to say. I was really over there buying time. Until he decided to bring his ass home. So many nights I sat and waited up. So many nights I sat on top of the kitchen table looking for familiar headlights. Or listening for a familiar sound that only his truck made. Most times the sun would beat him home. When I would hear his truck pull up. I would run into the bedroom and get in the bed acting like I was sleep. When he turned the bedroom door knob... I would rise from the covers and rub my eyes like I just woke up. That act was so obvious to me and to him. I wanted to argue and make my point. Instead, I cried and listened to bullshit excuses from him. An hour later I would be naked….glistening in the aftermath of awesome make up sex.

Bills were stacked high and money was not stacked at all. I started missing a lot of work. Either I was hung-over, no gas, or emotionally distraught. My work ethic was at a 0. It was hard to recognize myself in the mirror. My family life was there, they did a lot of things...parties, reunions and Sunday dinners. But I was a no show at just about everything. It's sad because no matter what, I can never get that time back. I dreaded going to work, and they dreaded me being there. Since I was so broke all the time, there were at least five people at work that I owed money too. I had made a new friend at work. She was an outside sales rep and she was super sweet too. She was smart, reliable and she too was in a relationship that couldn't be understood by outsiders. But her relationship didn't involve drugs. Often, we took lunch together. Or I would go over to her house and we would talk for hours. She believed in me. She wanted me to leave my lover just like everybody else did. She

Tamekia Nicole

became my confidant and I trusted her. But when she tried to advise me about my lover, I turned on her too.

Our relationship was obviously toxic ....even Ray Charles could see that. But I was hard headed. I never listened. Shit was hitting the fan on a more constant basis. We were drug addicts. There was never enough money to comfortably get high and still live life normally. One morning I left for work with no goodbye or kiss from him. I needed those in the mornings. Hell, I needed those all the time. That morning I was not going to be getting it. I never knew when to just let things go and move on. So, I decided to come home for lunch that day to discuss the previous day's altercations. In my gut I knew that something wasn't right. I couldn't explain it but I needed to go to home. So I went. I pulled up as quite as possible and went into the house. It was quite in there except for the loud echoes coming from the bathroom. It was him and he was on the phone. The acoustics in the bathroom make words crystal clear. I put my purse and keys in the spare bedroom. I crept to the bathroom, careful not to stand in the shadow of the gap from under the door. So he wouldn't see me before I was ready to be seen. The words and descriptions I heard from him about another woman made me physically ill.

On the phone with his cousin, my lover started talking about how smooth the girl's skin was. How pink the inside of her coochie was. How she smelled good, tasted good, and she was virgin. Holding my composure I kept on listening. He described and mimicked the sounds she made...as he gave her head in the back seat of his truck. He told his cousin that she was so fine. It made his dick hard thinking about her. "I never saw so much cream come out of one broad." Was his exact words. I was floored. I don't know is why I was floored. I knew who he was and what he represented. That was the man that he would always be. But it would be my choice of how long I would take the bullshit. I backed away from the bathroom door and went into the kitchen. I looked at the time and I needed to be back to work in 30 minutes. What I did next set the tone for many years to come. About what took precedence in my life. HIM vs WORK. He always won. I picked up the house phone, intending to listen to the remainder of the story. After about a minute or so...he thought he heard someone in the house. So I hung up. Scared to death. I decided right at that moment. I purposely would not be going back to work.

Love Made Me Do It

Tamekia Nicole

My lover came into that kitchen when he saw me, his facial expression changed. "Aye blood, let me call you right back Johnson is here." I looked at him and I started to go off, about how he didn't love me and how disgusting he was.

The next thing I know I had a sweltering black eye. "SO WHAT!" was his response in between blows, "You shouldn't have been listening to my conversation, nosey ass, insecure, bitch!" Ignorance is never bliss. In absolutely no way. We tussled, but he won. My eye was getting blacker by the second. I called my job and gave them an excuse, about why I wouldn't be back that day. When I came in to work that next day the atmosphere was quiet and eerie. I was scared. I fucked up. Instead of getting my money at a good job, I was trying to keep tabs on a worthless excuse for a man. "Tamekia?" "Can you come in here please?" I went into my manager's office and sat down. There was an envelope with my name on it. I knew that this was an exit interview. Enclosed in that envelope was my last check. Even though the ladies in my department didn't care for me, and weren't the friendliest. In hindsight they were able to see what I could not and would not see regarding him.

I was sad. Sniffling, and holding back tears I apologized I took my last check and went home. Now I had to tell this asshole that I had been fired from my job. I was unemployed with a black eye and a broken spirit. Pulling up to the carport, I wished that I had some sensational story to tell about getting fired. *Oh well, he isn't my daddy* was the best thought I could come up with. But I knew if I was too smart mouthed. He would whoop my ass like he was my daddy. I parked, grabbed my purse and looked inside the envelope. That check was $2,000. With that amount of money and the bills REALLY paid for the month. I knew that me and my lover would be too sky high to be fighting. He was a fiend and so was I. It's funny that I used to be scared of that word. How it used to cut me and make me feel like the scum of the earth. Everyone has had a demon or two. Drugs were my demon. I unlocked the front door as slowly as possible. When I turned the corner to go into the kitchen, he was there sitting, not doing shit. That was his daily routine. As much as I hated him and what we were becoming. I was glad to back home with him.

Tamekia Nicole

When we made eye contact. I immediately turned on the crocodile tears. They weren't fake tears, but I knew I needed to press them out fast and loud. Before, I had a matching set of black eyes. I sobbed in his lap and told them how they did me in. Failing... to mention the reason that for my termination. "Tamekia has been emotionally distraught, and unprepared to perform said job, at a satisfactory level." My lover didn't even ask about the reason. But he did ask if they cut my last check. I just handed him the envelope. His eyes lit up. Yeah life sucked. But the bullshit I was being force fed, would taste better once a little coke got in my system and I had the anxiety fucked out of me. Issues were never clarified, reasons never justified and problems never resolved. The drugs had us unconcerned and unbothered by real life issues. We were a mess. But tonight we would be a high mess. This was the difference between an awesome night....or a night of flying fists.

He grabbed his keys and to the bank we went. Now that there was more free time, I was hoping that it would be well spent with each other. If our time wasn't well spent, somebody may be dead by the end of the week. I honestly felt like it could be me. I would continue to hold on. I refused to call it quits. Black eye and all we would get thru this The scariest thing is, loving another person more than you love yourself. Fuck love, give me the drugs. The love I possessed was a gift and a curse. I was done crying I was ready to go get this dope. So, with my clearly exposed black eye, I went inside the bank. Cashed my check, lost my pride and tucked my dignity. We were off to go and buy as much drugs, as we could handle for the night. Life sucked ...but I would live off our cocaine high to get thru my dark moments.

CHAPTER 17

IT'S ALL ABOUT DRUGS

Tamekia Nicole

Even though it wasn't the most favorable situation, we had no choice but to make the best of a bad situation. I will say that everything wasn't all bad. But everything was far from good. In between the fights, the drugs, the make-up sex and the madness we did have some fun. We had a few parties. His friends and cousins would come over and we would we have a ball. I almost always drank too much, and spent most of my over the toilet. We woke up when we wanted to and then plotted on how to take over the world. When you use drugs, you are constantly thinking about your next move and using more drugs. We stayed high every day. We had so much time on our hands. As soon as we woke up. I gave him the money and he went and copped drugs.

Life was changing at such fast pace, I was fearful of the speed we were moving at. Since I was home all day, I had plenty opportunities to talk to my lover about any and everything. But usually after we used drugs, there wasn't too much conversation after that. I told my lover after he had copped about $100 worth of drug. That I wanted to roll the blunt for us, he was hesitant. But gave me all the tools I needed, the blunt, the weed, and the cocaine. He told me to break the cocaine down with the razor blade until it was powder like. That's when I asked him "If this is Coke, why is this like a rock?" That is when he told my naïve ass... that it was Crack. This whole time we were smoking Crack. My mama was going to kill me and for some reason using Coke sounded a little bit more respectful as a drug of choice. While I rolled this blunt he also warned me to never snort this type of coke. It would kill me. Life was full of surprises. Especially mine. *So all this time I have been smoking Crack? Did that make me a Crack head?* At that time I didn't think so, and I could find a million reasons why I wasn't a Crack head.

The number one reason was because there was no pipe involved. I thought in order to be that you had to be using a pipe. Like on New Jack City. I guess I didn't know as much as I thought I did. I sealed the blunt up, dried it off and sparked it up. At a minimum level we were smoking at least 10 blunts. On a maximum level, we smoked almost 40 blunts. It was a feeling that can never be explained. It's beyond powerful, that's why we mixed the Weed with it. To balance out the harshness of the drug. We made love, we kissed, we fought, and we used drugs.

Tamekia Nicole

He would put me out; throw my clothes out the front door. I would call my friends to come and get me. They would come and rescue me, but I would always go back. It was becoming obvious to others that something was wrong with me. I just told them that I was stressed. No one understood why I stayed with him, and neither did I. What I did know for sure. Is that it was hard for me to stay away from him. It was hard to stay away from the drugs. It was nearly impossible for me to consistently stay around my friends and enjoy their company. Everything was revolved around getting high and since they didn't use drugs, I barely seen them. I was becoming something that I didn't want other people to see. I was embarrassed, so I stayed away. They cared about me so much and they were so wonderful. I felt it was best for me to stay where I was at, in turmoil with him.

I'll never forget getting dressed one day to hang out with one of my girlfriends and my panties fell off of me. I had no idea how thin I really was. Everything in my closet slid off my thin frame. I had the figure of a snake. My existence was getting more shameful by the day. But I didn't care, it was me and my lover and fuck anyone else. As long as I was appealing to him....then whoever else didn't like it, could kiss my ass. He was getting thin too. His face was scared with acne, and there were lines that creased his face, that weren't there before. We slowly became people that we didn't even recognize. Sometimes when we would fight we would talk about how the other person looked. Our fighting was at an all-time high and more violent than ever. He asked me once "Where did your ass go?" I told him "The same place your dick went..." He slapped the shit out of me. Drugs had changed us they made him violent and kept me paranoid.

As if our situation wasn't already bad enough. He taught me a new bad habit. He taught me how to shop lift. I never stole anything in my life, but I wasn't opposed to it either. This whole time I was thinking that all his nice, material objects were acquired by working hard. No. He acquired those nice things with his sticky hands. I wanted nice expensive things too. Plus we needed an additional source of income to feed our growing addiction. Nothing was off limits.

Love Made Me Do It

Tamekia Nicole

Top shelf liquor was our biggest seller. We went in every store in our area, and it didn't matter if the items were behind the counter. He would take the bottles of alcohol we stole and trade them for dope. He was the business end of all the drug transactions. I was just the pretty girl that sat in his truck waiting to get high. My lover could take anything that was not nailed down. I was scared the first few times, but then it was fun. The only times that I was really scared, was when I felt like we were *hot* in a certain store. He was never scared, even if we were hot. We saved so much money since we stole everything. When we did grocery shop, he would push grocery carts out of the store filled with groceries. This was the life of drug addicts. We were barely functioning. I was incoherent most of the time and he was volatile. Pushing and shoving became normal. I expected it. I probably needed that verbal abuse just to feel alive. I was dying inside. If he wasn't physically abusing me, it was verbal.

As much as my body craved him, it was hard to make love with someone that beat your ass during the day. Then act like nothing ever happened. I never imagined this life, for myself. When my mama came to visit, I tried to act like things were normal. She told me not to move in there with him and so did several other people. But I didn't think I would be able to survive without him so I stayed. I repeatedly came back when he kicked me out. I was always reassuring people, that we were in love and things were fine. Things were far from fine. I wanted to die and I wanted to die high.

The drugs took the pain away they made things better and a little bit easier to manage. Once our hustle became better and I listened to him more instead of being argumentative. That made life a little bit better. It was the summer and I just wanted to have fun. Tension eased and we let up on using for a little while. I started getting dressed every day instead of lying around like his sex slave. We spent most of our good days going to the mall and stealing whatever our hearts desired. That summer seemed hotter than the average Bay Area summer. I remember driving around high as fuck when all of sudden I started feeling sick. I tried to tell my lover, let's just go home. But he said one more store we had one more store to hit. I never had a choice in what we did, unless he was broke. So I walked behind him in several stores. Getting impatient, I told him I need to go sit in the car. I felt weak. Finally, he was ready. We got onto an elevator full of people. I passed out. When I came too, I was no longer in the elevator. I was confused. I saw the look on my lovers face

Tamekia Nicole

and snapped out of it….Real quick. He helped me up and scolded me all the way to the car. He was pissed. I was pissed, that he was pissed. I told him I wasn't feeling good. Now my head was pounding.

Smoking Crack in extreme heat is a recipe for disaster. I called Kaiser and they advised me to come in, they thought I had a concussion. From hitting my head when I passed out. But I couldn't come in. I was scared that they would call the police about how high I was. So I made up an excuse. Excuses. I was becoming good at giving those. The advice nurse told me to stay up the whole night and monitor my pain. I was scared. I fucked up, now I had thoughts of dying of a concussion. Much to my surprise he encouraged me to go to the Dr. the next day. He said that I didn't look so good. So I went. Luckily, I was fine. When I came in the door he was lying across the bed. When he seen my face he jumped up and held me tight. No one would ever be able to fathom, the level of addiction we had for each other and the drugs.

CHAPTER 18

BACK TO WORK

Tamekia Nicole

Life was a little less miserable. Having all day and night with him was wonderful. But I couldn't just lay up every single day in a dark ass house. Getting fucked up. I know I was making plenty of mistakes, but my mama raised me better than that. So I landed another position at my last job's competitor. They loved me. I always had the ability to make friends especially at work. This place was no different. My coworkers would pick me up and bring me home whenever I needed. This became an all the time situation. I never had any money for gas because we spent it all on drugs. I saw $900 go in one night. When it was no stores open to steal from, and no more money, I got my ass whooped. Even though, I had went back to work. Money was still not like it was. So his nephew and his girlfriend came to stay with us.

It was cool, because when things were tense between the two of us there were others people, to interact with. I made a friend in the nephew's girlfriend. We used each other as needed. Half the time we only came out of our bedrooms when it was dark. At first I wasn't for sure if his nephew got high. But when he started riding shot gun to make runs, I knew he did. This was fine with me. It was nice to have the company in the house it made it feel more like a home. Versus a dark place, where bad shit happened. Although I was happier, my jealousy was at an all-time high. I was getting less attention now that the nephew was there. He was spending more nights out, with *places to go*.

So I tried to manage my time better. I was back at work. I conversed with the girlfriend here and there. I started reaching out to my friends. But it was all an act. I just wanted to be with him. I didn't want to talk or hang out with anyone else. I constantly was looking for ways to be sweet. His fish had recently died and he was apprehensive about getting more. So one day I surprised him and bought him some gold fish. But when he came home he was pissed at the sight of them. "Goldfish are dirty, and raggedy." I held my head down in disbelief. A few days went by and I caught him talking to the raggedy gold fish, while he was feeding them.

Tamekia Nicole

I was happy about that, but then I felt mad about it. He had just belittled me. He made my simple act of generosity feel unappreciated and stupid. So I killed those fish all nine of them. So now he couldn't complain or praise them. They were dead. He knew I killed those fish. But I lied with a straight face. He had taught me how to do that. So now I was a killer and a Crack Head. Life was a joke. My life was a joke. His temper was up and down. I had this crazy notion, that maybe I would get beat up less since we had roommates. That was wishful thinking. I was getting my ass whooped in our bedroom and no one rescued me. No one said shit to him. I felt like his nephew should have said something. But the nephew wasn't stupid, that was a battle he didn't want. Especially, because he needed a place to live. *Never bite the hand that feeds you.* The nephew stayed silent. The girlfriend stayed silent and I had been on mute. Sometimes we would be chillin' in the living room, and talking shit. My lover would start trippin' for no reason. I would just sit there and take it. If he thought too hard about anything, he could turn violent. There was no one to save me. But even worse I wasn't willing to save myself.

Money was getting extremely low. I had a gut feeling that I wouldn't keep my job for very long. I could barely stand to be away from him. This made going to work impossible. Plus I was extorting money from two of my coworkers and robbing them for anything that wasn't nailed down. I had picked up so many bad habits and mastered all of them. I was happy to have my own money. But in between him and the drugs I don't know which was harder for me to be away from.- Unemployment gave my lover the impression that there was still a nice amount left in that account. With the option to get two extensions if he needed too, to his surprise they stopped his checks. I was the only one in the house with a job.

The nephew had the audacity to tell me I was making too much noise in the morning. It went in one ear and straight out the other ear. Then he told my lover. I was choked shoved and advised to put my shoes on at the door, and not stomp thru the house with them on. *No good ass men...*were my only thought. I was sick of everyone in that house that had a penis. This living situation sucked. It was grueling, getting up every morning. While three other grown people stayed sleep. Something needed to change. I just didn't know how to make those changes.

Tamekia Nicole

Mold starting growing in our closet over a course of time. Times were getting a little rougher and Christmas was around the corner. My check seemed so small by the time bills were paid. The only thing I could treat myself to, was buying my lunch at work. Even that I had to hide. He owned me. His hustle income wasn't even enough for rent. Then the eviction notice came. It was on the kitchen table for days until it was looked at. What were we going to do.? We brainstormed collectively. With no solution, I felt like the world was on my shoulders. My lover and his nephew even plotted on robbing my ex roommate. That fell through, thankfully.

We had to give all our regular spots that we stole from a rest, before we went to jail. The icing on the cake was getting fired from my job. Times were hard as fuck. That was a hard one to swallow. I had it to good and I let it slip thru my hands. All behind a man and drugs. The devil was riding my ass, and God was nowhere in my sight. I just gave up. We were all pushed between a rock and a hard place. Having no money is the equivalent to no options. The mold spreading in our closet bought us time. His mom tried to pay everything but it was too late My family's door was always open, but there would be questions I didn't want to answer. No surprise that he went with his mama. The nephew went to Frisco I think. I went to my mom's house. That didn't last. Fitting in with my own family had long expired.

CHAPTER 19

MOVING AROUND

Tamekia Nicole

I went to my grandma's house thankful, to have a roof over my head. If it wasn't for her I would have been homeless. She said I was too thin. I was breaking hearts that I didn't even consider. I looked in the mirror, only to see a vague reflection of someone that I used to know. Myself. I was so skinny I could fit my 13 year old sister's clothes. But the best part about grandparents is that they nourish in a different way than mom and dad do. I was slowly getting back to a decent weight. Living at my grandma's house was good for me and could have been better if I knew how to stay in the house. My nerves were bad, anxiety high and my addiction was destroying my sanity. Without my lover I didn't know even know how to buy drugs for myself. *What did I say? Can I buy some Crack? Do you have any Crack for sell?* So I walked around depressed, getting fatter by the day. With me in San Jose and him in Stockton that was such a long distance. I didn't even have my car anymore. How in the fuck were we going to see each other? Why did I come back here and quit my job at American Express?

Even though we were miles apart…we managed to gravitate back to each other. The pull of the universe knew how deep our love was. We made a way out of no way to be together, only to have sex and get high. More often than not I would just spend the whole weekend with him. His mama still loved me. So I was more than welcomed there. We would rent DVD's and snuggle up in his bed. Where ever he was, I was right behind him. Using drugs slowed down a bit at least for me it did. There were too many family members in my business. Plus I had my baby sister looking up to me. I had to do better. He picked me up from my Grandma's for the weekend. He fired up that longest blunt I had ever seen in my life. We could smoke on that all the way thru the Altamont Pass and be good and blasted. It's crazy looking back at what we turned into and how fast it happened. We never talked about what was going on with us. How life was slipping right out of our hands. We rather watch Sponge Bob then talk about real life. Things picked up for him as well, living back at home. He gained his weight back, skin cleared up. Those crease lines disappeared. Erectile dysfunction seemed to get better. Even if none of that had changed I was not going to leave him. He even got a very good job.

Tamekia Nicole

Getting picked up regularly to spend weekends in Stockton with no gas money didn't last too long. My lover started making not so subtle hints about how I didn't have any money. It's funny how the tables had turned and now I was the broke one. He was too selfish to even buy me any of my necessities. So I stopped asking him for shit. I didn't need the extra grief. A little time had passed since we had stopped living together. During that little bit of time, I grew a small set of balls. I was tired of being treated like shit. So I adjusted my balls and said "Nigga please, you didn't have any money plenty of times and I had you x's 10." He took one look at me and slapped the shit out of me. The abuse rarely fazed me at that point. It was my new normal. I anticipated it after every disagreement or dry run to the ATM Machine. Those domestic violence classes he took, obviously did not change him. The rest of the way to Stockton was awkward. The music was too loud, it was uncomfortable.

Had I not been fearful of going to hell, I would have jumped out of car. Death by suicide. Thankfully, I decided not to jump out of the car because he just sparked up a blunt. *Just pass me the drugs and shut the fuck up.* Those are thoughts that never left my mouth, so they never reached his ears. Since he had an attitude and was feeling like *the man*. He took his sweet time passing the blunt to me. Instead of puffing and passing. He puffed the blunt until it was half gone. If I was brave enough to say something, about how long he was taking. I would risk not smoking at all. Finally, he passed it. I hated when he watched me while I smoked. *Fuck! Can I get high? You just slapped me damn, I need to decompress.* God forbid I hit the blunt too hard; he would snatch the blunt out of my hands. By the time we got to his house. I figured all was well. His body language was a little different and he hugged and kissed me. Okay, that's much better. Twenty's started pouring out of his pocket as he took his pants off. That solidified that our weekend would go very well. Money kept us happy, horny and high. Lack of money made us volatile, vindictive and vicious.

Love Made Me Do It

Tamekia Nicole

I hated leaving him on Sunday's that was the worst. Staring out the window, I would imagine that we were going on a surprise date instead of back to my grandma's house. That never happened though. I was still unemployed, and my Grandma definitely had something to say about how much I was running the streets. Instead of looking for a job, when she laid into me I just said okay. I took my ass to sleep, woke up early and started looking for a job. Instantly I was hired to do sales. That job and the people gave me the creeps they had too much energy at 7:30 in the morning. It was far away and they wanted me to wear tights and heels. No thank you. After my first check I was out of there. Instead of trying to explain to my grandma what my problem was. I went to live with my cousin in Stockton, just a few exits away from my lover. When she said I could stay there, I was taken aback. Our relationship growing up was more hate...than love. She had two bedrooms and was barely ever home. As sick as I was at that time, I should have stayed where I was at. I was severely addicted to drugs.

No one, who ever met my lover liked him. Thankfully there weren't many rules living with my younger cousin. Just the basic house rules, the number one rule was; no company especially him. Smoke and leave was the plan. Come over really quick, let's blow. Those were the instructions I had given my lover over the payphone. He came over all dressed for the day and here I was sitting in the house. With no phone and not dressed for anything but bed. Oh well, light it up. Once I get high nothing will matter. "Where did you get this?".... "That's that ooooooh wee" I held the smoke in, 'till my eyes rolled into the back of my head. Next thing I know I was naked and he was naked. He put a chair under the bedroom door knob as a lock. I rode him, he held me. In the midst of a position switch, I heard something or someone. I jumped up. My cousin was rattling the door knob trying to come in. My lover was getting dressed. When the door opened he was dressed. I was naked and the whole room smelled like coke. Rightfully so, my cousin went off and told me to get out. So I ran after him putting a piece of clothing with each step. Trailing right behind him to his truck. He closed his door and said "I ain't in this blood, you need to handle that." He sped off and I sat on the curb. Defenseless... In a situation that I created.

CHAPTER 20

NOW WHAT?

Tamekia Nicole

I sat for some time on that curb. Crying and trying to enjoy my high before it was all the way gone. Too late... All that commotion knocked the drugs out of my system. I walked to the corner picked up the phone and dialed my lovers home number. Knowing, that his mama would answer, she made him come back to get me and all my stuff.

That wasn't my ideal way to be with him for the weekend. But I rather that, than be homeless. It was obvious that he was dressed to be in the company of some bitch. He was pissed that he had to come back and get me. But he did and that was my only concern. He dropped me off at his mama's house and took off. He came back 15 minutes later, gave me hella crack, a pack of blunts, and a bag of weed. His mama was going to gamble out of town and he would be back. I went down stairs said thank you and good luck to his mama. What a day. I'm basically homeless, broke and on drugs. I loved the sound that a laced blunt made when you first lit it. I ran a hot bath with plenty bubbles. Turned the TV towards the bath tub, got my lighter, two blunts and a towel. I stripped down and sank into a temporary happy space. I allowed myself to sink down into the water just far enough to where a tiny bit of water seeped into my ears. With my feet on the faucet I blew clouds of smoke and contemplated my life. I could kill myself and be less of a burden to everyone around me. I really didn't know what to do. Or how to do it. But I knew for certain that I would not be staying here with him and his mama.

I just was caught smoking dope at my cousin's house after she welcomed me into her home. That was wrong. I have yet to live that one all the way down. Over the course of this journey I have learned to be accountable for every part of me. The good, the bad, and the ugly. I left guilt and shame behind me years ago. Wrinkled from head to toe, it was time to get out. I felt good in that moment alone with my own thoughts. Contemplating the next move for me. Drugs are not t compatible with, making calculated decisions. I just wanted to be with him.

Love Made Me Do It

Tamekia Nicole

The drugs were talking to me and I was listening only because I was dumb. I snapped out of my fog when I heard his truck. Partially naked and under the influence is how he found me. I must have been lying on the bed for hours after I got out the tub. The bed was damp, but I was dry and ashy. Internally he was fighting the urge to yell at me about making the bed wet and fucking up his weekend. Thankfully he spared me the bullshit argument. Instead he started tracing his fingers on different parts of my body. Every touch felt like a cold, wet paint brush that was searching for the perfect canvas to start a masterpiece. I closed my eyes, and closed off all the negative energy of the day's events. My lover began kissing my skin, which led to tasting my skin. Life sucked. I was homeless but his touch was the cure all. Making love was our only healthy connection.

I was dehydrated, hungry and ready to go to bed. We ate salami and crackers, and watched a movie until we fell asleep. In the morning I would deal with my problems. The morning came fast. I needed him to take me back to San Jose. Maybe I could go back to my Grandmas house. We dressed and headed to San Jose. Obviously he had things to do, people to see and places to go that did not require my presence. I put on yesterday's stale outfit with a new lease on life. "Where we going?", "Just drop me off at my Grandma's house, please" "Alright". No other words were said. No blunt had been mentioned or seen.

I folded my arms across my chest, and nestled into the r the passenger seat attempting to vibe with the music. We pulled up to my Grandma's house. I saw my uncle and my childhood friend in the driveway. Fuck. I do not want to see anyone right now. I leaned over and kissed him when he stopped the car. He said "Call me and let me know what is going on" I smiled and hopped out. Wasting no time I marched in the house, and sat at the dining room table with my Grandma. Rumors and half-truths had already surfaced about the incident at my cousin's house. Just as I knew it would. Grandma was easy on me. Although no one directly asked me if I was using drugs it was heavily implied. I needed to be serious about getting it together. So I got a job at a psychiatric facility. I went to that job every day and put forth my best effort. I had done too much, and getting my priorities straight was no longer an option it was a necessity. My family was beyond disappointed in me. I just wanted to get things back to normal. Even if, that meant not talking to him for a period of time

Tamekia Nicole

My snake figure began looking more like its original form…..curvy. He was doing well from what I could gather from our brief phone calls. We made love when and wherever permitted. Not seeing each other as often was good for us. I was lost and so was he. I was still dealing with the situation with my cousin. No matter how many times I would try to pull her to the side so we could talk….she started talking loud and calling me names. So I let it go. I knew what happened, but she had exaggerated the story in such a way, that nothing I said mattered.

So I proceeded in showing everyone that I could be better. I avoided his calls, so that I could focus. I was making good money and started saving for another car. I was getting up early and getting on the bus and going to work at the ass crack of dawn. I was on a mission to prove people wrong. I had been relying on the drugs and him for far too long. You can only cheat your body and brain for so long before it shuts down. It had been about a month or so since I saw my lover. I actually had direct instructions from my family not to see him. Or I had to get out. So I adhered to those rules. I had too. But then I started to sneak and see him again. I started missing work or showing up late. I would tell my family that I was going out of town to Reno or LA. But I would really be with him. His family didn't care, but my family did.

I would catch the train to spend the weekend with him. That way no one saw him picking me up. Plus it was easy on his gas tank and our pockets. There was no tension in the air, because we both had positive things going on in our life. Tonight felt like the old days. My soul was recharged, my spirit renewed. Before any drugs were brought out we hugged. Resting my head on his shoulder, we hugged. That was another moment that I wanted to bottle up for those long dreary days that came along. Talking, oh my God I can't believe how much we talked that night. Our new jobs, what we've been doing, did we miss each other and everything in between. This was my friend, my lover, a man I once knew and the man I wanted to always know. Happiness was an expression I missed seeing on his face. Shit, I missed being happy too. Experiencing happiness at the same time was the best part about the whole weekend. No drugs were mentioned but when the conversation was almost dead. He reached under his bed and pulled out our extra dose of happy. Drugs. Crack to be exact, now there was no weed to mix it with. Now we just would save some of the tobacco filling and mix it in with the cocaine. Lift off. I loved to be with him. I loved to be high with him.

Tamekia Nicole

Money was flowing from legitimate sources so we didn't have to go out and rob stores. We talked about living together again now that we were getting back on our feet. I knew my family wouldn't approve, especially because what the drugs and him had already done to me and my life. I had a decision to make.

For the time being life was pretty content. I was doing very well at my job. Then I was laid off. Fuck! But this time I was prepared. I had a few thousand saved up. The cat was out the bag about my lover and I being back in contact. I just told my family to deal with it. I loved him and that would always be. With no job I had ample amount of time and money to spend with him. I would spend days on end at his house. Using drugs, and catering to his every need. We were a very harmonious space….until everything changed. If I kept my mouth closed about his suspicious behavior we would have gotten along much better, for longer periods of time. But I noticed everything. This was something that he couldn't stand. But I didn't give a fuck. Stop disrespecting me and there would never be a problem. I needed to take my life more seriously. It was a must that I started making better decisions for myself or else I was going to die. We would see each other here and there. Until, I started acting funny with him. I didn't really want to be bothered anymore. I liked having money in my pocket that wasn't being spent 100% on drugs. I was scared of myself and I was even more scared of myself when I was with him.

It was like there was no limit to the things I was willing to say yes too. No person should have that type of effect on another person.

CHAPTER 21

MOVING ON

Tamekia Nicole

Talking to my grandma and listening to her struggles growing up. I began weaning myself away from him and the drugs. That shit was so hard. Some night I felt like I was going to rip someone's head clean off their shoulders. Some nights I gave in and every time I did, I would be so sick from the drugs. I would start throwing up and sweating. One time my baby sister had to call 911 because I couldn't stop vomiting. They threw me on the ambulance and asked me what I had that day and did I take anything. To ashamed I never said one word. I just complained that I was in pain. Too many irresponsible nights that led into an irresponsible week. Fuck that, I had to put those days and him in my rear view and I did. Living at home started getting much better, because I was turning back into myself. The *Meka* that everybody loved. That felt good.

I was in the neighborhood where I grew up. So I still had a lot of my same friends that were just around the corner. I spent my evening unwinding in my hood with my childhood friends. Everyone was so happy to see me. I felt like I was a celebrity. Most night's I would lie in my bed and think about why I allowed drugs get to me like that. Drugs were the devil and they were still calling me. The volume wasn't as loud as it had been. But it was loud and clear. So I started popping pills and doing a few lines here and there. Those were more acceptable drugs to buy in my own neighborhood. Everybody was doing it and as long as I wasn't getting huge quantities. I would be under the radar. I needed to fill a void inside of me that only drugs could fill. I had become a closet addict. No one knew how serious it was for me even the ones who thought they knew me best.

Against my better judgment I called my lover. Just like all the other times when we hadn't spoke for a while. It was a little weird and perhaps even a little dry but I didn't give a fuck. He belonged to me when I wanted it and vice versa. An hour and a half later he was picking me up on the side of my house. I hopped my ass in that passenger seat leaned in and kissed him. I held the side of his face to let him know it was real and that I needed him. I hoped to God that he needed me too. He took off for the hills behind my house; he had a blunt already rolled.

Tamekia Nicole

I loved the smell of cocaine burning in the air. The windows were fogged up and I was naked telling him to get in the back of the truck with me. We literally stayed naked, sweaty and high until the sun started coming up. I was satisfied and shaking. Being too high isn't good when you have taken a break. Your heart can't take the starting and stopping that's how the most damage is done.

He dropped me off on the side of the house and waited until I was in the house. Then he turned up his beat and took off down the street. An hour or so later I started throwing up all over the place. I told my sister to call 911. Obviously, I was not built for this lifestyle. This time I was picked up from the emergency room, by my grandma. She didn't let me off the hook that easy, I was lectured all the way home. No need to say anything back because I knew it would only be lies. I was tired of lying. All the other areas of my life were pretty squeaky clean accept when it came to him and things I did with him. I took head to those words that came from my grandma. I stopped taking all calls from him. My friends were back in rotation. I was running the streets and looking damn good while doing it.

I met some-one that I heard had the "juice" with the girls. Supposedly a ladies man, so I was going to see what he was all about. I shall call him the "jack rabbit" for years to come that name will be very relevant in my life but in the end he was a sorry ass nigga just like the ones before him. The jack rabbit was in my extended circle and there was plenty women who knew him. So I tried my luck. We would spend hours on the phone and we started getting close. I would take out of town trips with him to pick up and drop off duffle bags. So now that I wasn't using drugs, bad boys became my high. The thrill in life is what made my blood pump. The jack rabbit had a level of shadiness that hung over his head. But for the most part it never bothered me. I was excelling at work; my family life was back in tact so I kind of didn't care. Party's came and went. I just continued to make sure that I was in appearance looking my best. My lover and I were barely on speaking terms and that was fine with me. I was too busy for the bullshit anyway. Sometimes it bothered him that he couldn't get ahold of me and sometimes it bothered me. But it

Tamekia Nicole

was what it was. So after a few weeks of phone tag, on a lonely night I decided to give my lover a call. He didn't answer.

So I carried on with the rest of my night. My neighborhood friends were a good pick me up. As I walked around the corner, I thought to myself...*where is this nigga at? If you wanted to talk to me so bad then why didn't you answer the phone?* I sat down in the garage with my friends. This was what life was about, friends that turn into family. My phone starting ringing in my pocket it was like 1am. I pulled out my phone my heart started beating out of control. It was my lover...but now I had an attitude and didn't' want to talk. So I didn't answer. Then he called two more times. I answered on the 2nd call, with an attitude. I recall the conversation going like this. "Hello...yeah, what's up?" "Oh where are you at?"..... "I'm in my neighborhood." "No you're not; you're at some nigga's house." This conversation was going nowhere fast. So I hung up on his ass. When he called back I let my friend answer the phone. My lover started asking my friend hella questions. I gave my friend the cue to hang up the phone. He called back and I answered the phone. This was the back and forth that we went thru all the time. It was the sickest love, that I ever seen yet alone been involved with. So we did the back and forth on the phone, while I sat in a garage full of my homies.

Then my lover dropped a bomb on me "That's why I fucked her," I was speechless to say the least. Here was karma coming back for me in the worst way. So I fucked your best friend and you go and fuck a girl that was my friend. I listened and tried to think of an appropriate response. But all I could do was cry and hang up the phone. I stayed in the garage with my homies until about 4 in the morning feeling sorry for myself. I was embarrassed that I was constantly riding an emotional roll coaster. So I walked back to my house drunk and riddled with shame and guilt. He fucked her, and I fucked his friend maybe we could just be even now. Maybe with God's help we could move forward.

Tamekia Nicole

That was purely a wishful thought. Lying in my bed I started thinking about my life once again. None of those thoughts made me happy. I had the jack rabbit on deck but my heart belonged to my lover. I didn't think that was ever going to change. Morning time came. I did an internal check, to see where my emotions were at regarding the news that I heard the night before. I was still hurting. So I decided to give her a call. I paced around the house with an attitude. I needed to get some shit off of my chest with this broad. I opened up my phone and began searching for her name. I still had it. I hit talk once I got to her name. She answered on the second ring. The conversation became so ugly. She told me that he had been her man and that she was going to come to my house and whoop my ass. At first I was totally speechless. Listening to how much of my business that she really knew.

Just a few months back she wanted to be a permanent fixture in my life. I didn't want any parts of that she was nothing but a headache. We went back and forth. But at the end of the day I was just a fool on my front lawn going off on a broad that wanted me...but wound up fucking my soul mate. They were both a waste of time and a waste of my energy. I put that situation on the back burner and tried to focus on my party life, my friends and of course the jack rabbit. The jack rabbit was small in stature and in the bed. But the jack rabbit had me content for that moment. They say the best way to get over someone is to get underneath someone else. We hung out, and had sex. But it wasn't enough to really solidify it as a real relationship.

At 25 I felt like I needed more in a relationship, at least something that had substance. As much as I loved men I couldn't properly digest all the stress that came with that territory. A man was like a full time job with no pay. That's probably why my history will show you, that it was very rare that I kept both at the same time successfully. The jack rabbit was still in my life and things were going well. The sex was average, sometimes it was really good depending on if we were getting along or not. The saying goes "It's not the size of the boat but the motion in the ocean." They lied. I don't care how good the motion is, if the penis is small like the one that he had. It's the love that makes it feel good. Years and years down the line his small penis became the joke of me and my friends. He was one of the stingiest lovers I've ever had. But no one is perfect and for that moment and many moments after that. I loved him. Loving has never been a hard thing for me to do. I either love a person or I dislike

96

Tamekia Nicole

them. Once I love you, I just always love you. When loving another person it has to be for real. That other person has to know it. Some people can handle that type of love and to others it's foreign and scary. The jack rabbit started doing disappearing acts and not showing up where he was supposed to be, when he was supposed to be there. One of the last times he spent the night at my house. He had a gun hidden underneath my bed. I was so pissed. I woke his ass up and asked him... "Why in the fuck would you bring a gun to my grandmother's house?" He didn't say one word he just took his gun and got dressed and left.

So at that moment I knew that I had to take a few steps back from him. It was pretty easy after a week of no talking and thinking about that gun incident. I was in and out of contact once again with my lover. When we were in contact, the sex was amazing the getting high was amazing. So, since I was on hiatus from the jack rabbit. I was a little more attentive to what my lover was doing and could we do it together. My lover was receptive to my flirting. We were in a lot of hotels, motels and his good mama's house. Obviously it was not going to be long, before we were at each other's throat. The jack rabbit never had a chance when my lover, was in close proximity. I was torn between two men that were no good for me. One was just a little safer.

CHAPTER 22

I ONLY KNOW THAT THIS IS HELL

Tamekia Nicole

Disappearing acts had become quite regular with me. No one was too surprised when they started happening again. I couldn't help it. I was really on drugs and I was really in love. Even to this day love scares the shit out of me, because I am still learning to enforce my personal boundaries. I was disappearing with my lover. I was no longer talking to the jack rabbit and ignoring my friends. I was only sleeping at home two to three times a week. I was getting bad. We fought. I got clean. We made up. I started using. There were good times. But there seemed to never be a choice for me.

Either I prayed for the wrong thing...or there was a lesson that I had yet to learn. Something had to give. Well I wasn't broken yet so I guess I would hang in there a little while longer. I started living with my lover at his dear mama's house. Only she didn't know. To be honest, I am not even sure how I wound up living there. But I know it was hell, a hell that I put myself in. Living in a house full of people without them knowing, was pretty hard. There were foster kids living there and they were young and nosey. We slept all day, and the good thing is that no one ever knocked on his door when they knew he was sleep. So for about a month or so, we just chilled. Ate hella food, went on drug binges, and fucked like wild animals. All, under his mama's nose, she never had a clue that I was there. Some nights we would be so high and horny that we would go out and watch the prostitutes on Wilson Way in Stockton. We would watch and talk the hoes that we saw getting in and out of cars. I was fascinated. I had never seen a hoe in real life. It looked scary. Watching the hoes car hop turned him on.

I could only imagined where this new found fetish would take our relationship. Our biggest issue was the lack of money. The lack of money only equaled black eyes for me and no high. Out of disparity on a cold, dark ass night he dropped me off across from an old bar. On a side street in Stockton and told me not to call him until I have money. If I never called he would kill me. When I refused to get out the car, he simply said. "You've fucked for free." So I got out. He threw two rubbers on the seat. I wiped my tears and closed the door. Here was my opportunity to run. Here was my opportunity to call for help. The only opportunity I had and I didn't take it.

Tamekia Nicole

I looked around trying not to panic. I don't know what exactly I was looking for. I didn't even know what I was going to say exactly. I just hoped that nobody killed me out here. But if they did I hoped that it would be quick and fast. I walked around trying to look normal, that's when a truck caught my attention. He was signaling for me to come over to him. I was so scared. But I got in the truck. He was old and creepy and he wanted a hand job. I didn't want to touch it or him. It was small, wrinkly, and pale. I hoped that he killed me. I put my hands around his dick and started a really fast jerking motion with my left hand. Tears raced down my face.

My lover knocked at the window, and told me to get out. He asked me where the money was. I handed it to him and I followed him back to our truck. That is one of the worst days of my life. Often people ask me why I stayed, why did I take so much? I thought you were supposed to stick by a person no matter what. That's what loyalty was. That wasn't loyalty that was stupidity. There were many days when he wouldn't let me eat. He would eat right in front of me and not offer me shit. I started losing more weight and I was being dropped off on a corner damn near every night. The corners were filled with a bunch of cut throat hoes that really had to do this to survive. I was too cowardly to break away from the abuse and the drugs. I would rather go out in public and proposition a stranger for sex, than get my ass beat. He dropped me off on different corners and I was expected to come back with money. I swear he watched too many pimp movies. It didn't really work that easily. I met a few girls along those few months that taught me a few tricks to get over. I also met girls who tried to get me to come home with them to their "daddy".

There were the girls who were run-aways, girls who made a lot of money… there were girls who were on drugs, and then there were girls whose dudes made them do stupid shit. I fell into a few categories. I would be lying if I said I made all this money. But I will be telling the truth, when I say I was getting the shit beat of me when I made no money. I was out there to get enough money for us to get high that night. I was snuck in and out of his mama's house and I only ate when he felt like giving me food.

Tamekia Nicole

There was a train table in his room and that is where I slept... Under, the train table. The train table circumference was smaller than that of a twin bed. So you can imagine how small and tight that space was. Unless, he was being nice or wanted to have sex I stayed under there. It was rare that I even wanted to be touched. I felt so disgusting, so ugly, and so worthless. Unless he said it was okay. I did not come from under that table. I peed under that table in plastic red cups. When it was time to go out and make money he let me shower. I put a piece of paper in my pocket every night that had my mother's name and phone number on it. *If you find me please call mother.* It was a real scary situation that I had gotten myself into. I hoped that someone would kill me. Some nights I begged God that someone would kill me. I was sleeping with strange men for money and had a drug problem. That was progressively getting worse.

The tricks that I picked up were creepy, and needy. There was the white supremacist that breathed so heavy. I just knew that he was going to kill me. Half of his upper body was covered in racial slurs and logos. There was the highway patrol that picked me up on Christmas Eve that was beyond creepy. There was the man that wanted me to urinate on him and I couldn't. But I did manage to drip hot wax on him, and hog tie him with the stereo cord. He really liked that. Then finally there was the man who caught asbestos cancer and wanted to talk all night. He gave me $500. My lover took that money and left me in a motel 6 room with a half a quarter piece of dope. I didn't see him till the next day well after check out time. This routine went on for about two months or so. It was never easy. Oh! How could I forget the man that gave me the counterfeit money and the dude who tried to kill me? But whenever I complained or cried. I either was beat up, denied drugs or was laughed at. I stayed under the table like a well-trained animal. Some days he would be gone the whole entire day 8 hours or more. There weren't even any sounds from a T.V for me to listen too. No food aroma for me to whiff. Just silence. Sometimes his mama would come in and sit on his bed, and talk on the phone for hours. I would be two feet from her scared to even move, let alone breathe.

Tamekia Nicole

I felt disgusting and I am sure I looked it. He had hit me so hard a few nights prior it was hard to walk. I was damn near paralyzed. But yet I had no bruises. He was becoming a professional. He didn't even need to leave a mark in order to cripple me. How in the fuck was I going to get myself out of this situation? God always made a way. I just had to listen this time. This night was kind of special we had a bunch of money and he went and copped a bunch of drugs. I felt kind of good. I could smoke away my problems and ignore how gross I had become. Shortly after dividing up the drugs he said he would be down stairs watching a porno. This was fine by me. I rolled four blunts loaded with crushed up Crack. As I started smoking the 2nd blunt I started hearing some moaning from down stairs. I was thinking to myself....*damn can you turn the damn T.V down.* I realized that it wasn't the T.V when I heard a woman's voice cry out my lover's name. I immediately got up, tucked my drugs in my bra and started getting dressed. He heard me. He raced up the stairs and told me to lay the fuck down and roll another blunt. I wasn't going to be doing either.

I charged past him, trying to see who the girl was. I never saw her. When I got close to the front door he opened it up and booted me out on the porch. I had no jacket and was wearing a mini skirt, sandals, and a thin ass tee shirt. I had a shoulder bag with my wallet, a box cutter and my flat iron in it. Those were the only things I owned. The wind chill was barely tolerable. I was shivering as I took a razor blade to the side of his truck. WHORE. That was the best word to describe him. Stupid as fuck are the best 3 words to describe me. I ran away. But, not far enough. He found me. He actually found me twice. The 1st time he found me. He kicked in a friend of mine's front door. He let me live that time because she had a new born baby in the house. Or I would have been dead. The 2nd time he seen me I was walking and he spotted me and drove up on the sidewalk and tried to run me over. I was way off into an area of life that I was unfamiliar with. But I did know. That it was survival of the fittest.

CHAPTER 23

BIG MAMA'S DAY CARE

Tamekia Nicole

I finally made my way back to San Jose. I slept over a friend of mine's house so I could have the chance to think about where I was going to go. I needed to get my shit together. I had no other choice but to go to my grandmother's house. I was well rested, but there was no way to hide the fact that I was skinny. I was so thin. It was disrespectful to my-self and to others. It was heartbreaking to think about those times in my life. I was a total let down. I knocked at the kitchen window and she came and let me in. I started crying and she just hugged me. I said "Grandma, I don't have anywhere to go, can I please stay here...I'll do better I promise?" She told me that she had a daycare and that she would have to see if it was okay. Ultimately she let me stay.

I can't believe how disrespectful we can be as human beings, myself included. When I think back at how many people really had my back. I could never consider being disrespectful to any of them at this point in my life. I always turned into the fat and happy Meka when I was at my grandma's house. I was relaxed and motivated. That same song and dance I was doing was old. I was almost 30 years old. Life was creeping up on me faster than I anticipated. I felt free. I hadn't felt that in a long time. The majority of the reason was because I was away from my lover. Plus I wasn't using. The remaining was my will-power. A good job was never hard to acquire. Back on pace... I had a job, bought a lil' bucket and life was starting to get good again...well more like decent.

Everyone was little bit less suspicious of me. Questions did not stop. I could barely pee in peace. However, it was gestures like that, that helped pull me out of the hell that I was in. Those gestures stuck with me and always will. My attitude was up and down. Detoxing from drugs would sometimes take a toll on me. Those drugs really fucked up the part of my brain that processes happiness. Drugs fucked up your life and they can fuck up the lives of your loved ones. Those drugs did all that to my life and I'm just now starting to get it back. Maintaining a good attitude was mandatory at my grandma's house. I wasn't paying any bills. So I walked around smiling or I stayed in my room.

Tamekia Nicole

I re introduced myself back to my friends. Hoping to be forgiven, luckily I was always welcomed back. Allowing them to see me while I was "sick" was hard for me. But since I loved them so much I wanted to be around them. And not miss out. I partied, I chilled, I drank. I fucked around with jack rabbit...again. Then it started again, it had been at least 2 or 3 months since we had spoken. My lover called and said that he was moving to Vegas. I had heard that before. But I listened to the fake dates and fake plans. I was tired of him. Oh my God, I swear he was like the Devil. Every time I tried to shake his ass....he was back. However, I knew he wasn't the Devil. Close, but not the Devil. That Crack Cocaine was the Devil. My Lover was just his right hand man.

CHAPTER 24

HE MOVED

Tamekia Nicole

He really moved and he called me from fabulous Las Vegas. I felt some type of way about the move. I just don't know what that feeling was. It was nice that he was away. With my lover out of the way, maybe now I could breathe. If the Lord didn't save me now... I didn't want to be saved. Period. My same routine was back in full effect. Family, friends, work, parties and normalcy. I was going to fight to keep from fucking this up. That actually worked for a little while. I was normal. I was involved with my family, I was working, I was taking care of my business and I was hanging with my friends. I swear that's all I wanted out of life. But when the drugs started calling me I answered. Then low and behold, my lover was always calling in on the other line. And vice versa. They had me. Fuck... I should have just kept minding my business and staying away from his. He invited me to come for a visit to Vegas. Against my better judgment, I went.

I literally told a million lies just to get out of town, without anyone knowing where I was going and who I was going to see. This was a rough way to live life. But logic was never a friend of mine. Landing in Vegas had me overcome with emotions. As soon as I spotted him in the airport, I ran straight to him. This was an amazing feeling. He was amazing. How I managed to stay away from him this long was beyond me. I hugged and grabbed his hand and interlocked our fingers. This was the shit I lived for. This is who I lived for. There was no concern as to what we were going to do or when. I just knew that we had a lot of cash to burn and we could fuck until the sun came up. There was no sneaking or any of that. I called home and let them know I had landed safely in "Reno," and I would see them in a few days. With my phone shut down, nobody was going to ruin this weekend. As soon as he took my bags and I settled in, I gave him hundreds of dollars to get us some drugs. My lover kissed me and said he would be back. It had been almost six months since I had gotten high. This was going to be wonderful.

When he came back I was showered, naked, and wet. He immediately set up the drugs. Dividing it up so that we could each have our own blunt, then he set up the video camera and a tri pod. It was definitely going down. This was my type of party. His touch woke my body up. It made my soul tingle. Those drugs....Man those drugs had me wide open. Down for whatever for him. Never, ever against him. I never saw the famous Las Vegas strip that weekend. But I did reconnect with my soul-mate. We had become one. The next few weeks were hard for me. I missed my lover so much it was ridiculous. However we had a plan.

The plan was for me to come out there and start a new life. We were going to get married and finally have a baby. So I carried on with life in California and saved up my money. Things at my grandma's were okay. The only thing I did was plot on how fast I could see and be with my lover. Nothing else mattered. Friendships shifted. Irresponsibility kicked in. Absenteeism was prevalent. My next trip was by bus, all the way to Vegas. That was not a good travel experience. The bus broke down and my phone wasn't working. But I didn't give a fuck. I would walk to see him if I had too, and by the time I got to his door step. 3 hours past the original time... I had looked like I walked there.

This was my baby. Even though my family thought that I was in "Lake Tahoe," I was going to work on weaning him back into their good graces. Right now we were working on us, we were figuring out how to get us right. He had yet to get a job and I had been wiring him money left and right. Life was good for me financially, probably because I wasn't paying that many bills or using. Same routine, I got settled in and gave him hundred dollar bills. He went and got us some drugs. I told him to get enough for the whole entire weekend. So there would be no interruptions. He did as he was told. Every day was a slice of heaven. In the bed, all day with the love of my life nobody could give me better than this. He came back with more than enough. We rolled our separate blunts. Crushed Crack, and a little Tabaco. I smoked until my ears rang, and my crotch throbbed. This stuff was so powerful that I didn't care about anyone including myself.

He shared the house with his older brother, who could not stand me. But because his brother loved me there wasn't shit he could do to get rid of me. I loved that. But yet in still I made friendly conversation with his family. Even, with the ones who did not like me. This was everybody. His mama could no longer stand me. But guess what? I didn't give a fuck. He loved me, so until he said otherwise I wasn't going anywhere. We ordered in and kept to ourselves. The only disturbance was his brother saying that there was smoke coming out of our room. We adjusted the towel under the door and went back to what we were doing. Each other. My grandma was getting re-married that weekend. Everyone's only concern was that I get back in time for the wedding. I was part of the

Tamekia Nicole

bridal party. I cried so hard when he took me to the greyhound station, it was unbearable to let go. Back, on the hot ass bus. Away from my heart beat.

I had a lot to think about on this bus ride. How was I going to pick up my whole life and place it in Las Vegas? How was I going to tell my family and friends? Although, I was madly in love I needed to make this as strategic of a move as possible. This was going to be next to impossible because things never went according to plan when my lover was involved. I went on with life, making sure that I was giving my lover most of my time as well as most of my money. He was so slow to change and partly because I was an enabler. I stifled some of his growth. Every month was a different reason or excuse as to why he did not have any money, or needed more money. I knew him all too well at this point. Hustler, con artist, cheater, and a womanizer, you name it...he mastered it. Especially when it came to me, it was a cold world and yet I was the only one who ever needed a jacket. Everyone else in the world was prepared but me. My way of living was definitely hurting other areas of my life.

I could count on my lover for very few things, but I could definitely count on him to fuck things up. Especially when everything was going so well between us, everything he did started to become a turn off. He was not working. He had no mode of transportation, he was selling candy bars for extra money, and he was smoking Crack. After settling back in at home and once again listening to what my grandmother was trying to teach me about life, love and possessing a decent work ethic. I started to feel stupid. I felt embarrassed and started having the mind-set that he was below me. My lover was below me. I felt bad for even thinking that. But I think it may have been true.

Even from Las Vegas, he was stressing me out. So I put him on the back burner. I was tired of sending money, the drunken calls, the belligerent texts and the whining. He was a grown ass man. He wasn't acting like it. Two children had no business being in any type of situation with one other. So I said my goodbye's and told him that I couldn't do this anymore. I stopped caring and I hung up the phone. While he was sleepless and sorry as fuck in Las Vegas. I was doing everything that was needed of me in order to show my family that things had changed for me. I was not using as much drugs as I was when I was with or around him. But I wasn't squeaky clean either. The only difference between a Coke

Tamekia Nicole

habit and a Crack habit is that one is a little, tiny bit more manageable. Both are bad news. Both can have you on the news... So I dibbled and dabbled, a few lines here, and there with old friends. I put the jack rabbit back up on deck and that was life. I had sex pretty regular although his "small" ways were more than likely to be a disappointment. I rocked with him. I loved the jack rabbit, and I'm sure that he loved me right back.

However, the jack rabbit was grimy and could not be trusted. He was in the life and I was never ready for that life style. It only sounded good in a rap song. But... could I really live that life? I knew that I couldn't but I tried anyway. I stayed down. I didn't ask too many questions. I deposited bogus checks. I answered all the calls that came from him. I played another stupid role, with a stupid dude. I was stupid. Men had that effect on me. They used to have that effect on my mama. She broke her cycle. I had to break mine.

CHAPTER 25

SURPRISES

Tamekia Nicole

He surprised me by showing up in California, he as in my lover. He sounded like he was in the car so I asked him. "Where are you?" He said "I'm on 580." I was thinking to myself CALIFORNIA? What in the fuck was he doing here? He said he wanted to see me too. I wasn't prepared to see him but he was my lover. So to some extent I would always be ready for him and how he needed me. Thru the fights, the funk, the love, the breaking up, the making up and fucking each other's friends….we were holding onto this unhealthy love. Love was making us do it, once again. So I got all pretty and was ready to see him. I was ready to let go and more so I was ready to get high. I knew that hadn't changed. Drugs were now a part of who we had become. I felt that I was strong enough to weather any storm that he may bring. Along with any questions he may have in regards to what I had been doing and who I was doing it with. I remember driving down 680 with the anticipation of seeing the one who held my heart. We met in Fremont. I parked my car and jumped in his truck. We drove along the hills in the Sunal Grade and passed a blunt back and forth. It had been a minute since I smoked anything. I had been snorting Cocaine here and there but that didn't give me the rush that this did. Or maybe it was him that gave me the rush.

Usher's confession was playing and I positioned myself in the car so that I had my legs on the dash board. He couldn't keep his eyes off of me and I matched his stare. No matter how long it had been, he had the capability to mesmerize me. I felt a little woozy after I hit that blunt. This is how it was with my body and those damn drugs. I should have just said no. Those drugs and him would be the death of me. If I let them. We talked. I asked him what he was doing here and told him next time don't sneak up on me. I don't like that shit. He laughed and so did I. There was no point in that statement. He only said that he had a court date out here and that he was here to handle some other business. So I sat back and enjoyed the rest of the blunt and the ride. I was so nervous that he was in town. I needed to make adjustments and I needed to make them quick. I was seeing the jack

Tamekia Nicole

rabbit and I needed to make sure that he didn't come along unannounced. I also had a bouquet of 2 dozen roses at my house that I would need to move out of eye sight. Just in case my lover decided to come over.

He looked so good and smelled even better. This would be the night that would change my life. After he dropped me off to my car I couldn't stop thinking about him. I wanted him now, more than ever. Those few trips that I made to Vegas to see him, didn't serve the complete purpose. I needed him. All of him. The next night I told him to come over and spend the night with me and bring plenty to smoke. That whole day at work, I couldn't think of anything but him. He was taking over my whole thought pattern. I was drawn to him like rays to the Sun. I couldn't wait another second for him to make love to me. To take me places that other men could never take me. Willingly he did so. We spent the night at my house. We were sprawled across each other. This felt so right but I knew that it was so wrong. It became increasingly hard to concentrate at work, due to my reintroduction to the drugs and to him. So I made it simple on myself. I took a few days off of work so that I could chill with him, make love to him and intoxicate his whole entire body. He was due to go back to Vegas after his court date. So our time was limited and I wanted to give him as much attention as I could. Before, I had to go back to work.

He never went to court, even though he insinuated that he was. He asked could use my phone for that day. He had to pay his phone bill; he would see me after work. Reluctantly, I gave him my cell phone. As soon as I got to work I called anyone and everyone who I thought may call or text me that day. I told them not to contact me. I kept calling him that whole day, checking on him and my phone. I cared more about him looking thru my phone, than his legal issues. The last time I called to check on him, is when he told me that he was too scared to go to court. So he didn't. I tried to console him and give him justifications of why that was okay. It really wasn't though, it was dumb and irresponsible and I had left that life behind.

Tamekia Nicole

But as we know by now there are no rules when it comes to my lover. We do what feels natural. Natural felt so right, so how could it be wrong? I was getting sick again, and I didn't know if I was willing to throw another good job away for the sake of a love, that could never be guaranteed. I was so tired of learning hard lessons. But obviously not tired enough. All of a sudden I stopped showing up for a job where I was the manager. They said I self-terminated. I was caught once again in a drug fog that would not allow me to see anything past, chasing a high.

According to research a Crack Cocaine high only last (4) seconds and you keep getting high. Trying to achieve the first high you've ever had. You will never even get close. So here I am for the umpteenth time, no job, strung out on love and drugs. This was a deadly combination. Honestly, I didn't know if I would survive this go round. I didn't want to tell my family, that I had lost another behind my lover. Who as far as they knew, he was living in Vegas. Too many lies. Too much stress. I had no idea what I was going to do now that the smoke had cleared. I couldn't keep pretending to go to work every day. I couldn't get high every day. I know that he could, but I had steered clear of the lifestyle and yet again it was in my face. What the hell was I going to do? Home life was just okay. My grandma had recently remarried and sold the house to my uncle. That transition took more out of me then I realized that it would. I was so spoiled and used to the nurturing that my grandma gave me. I could barely function with her gone. Every time I stepped into the kitchen I started crying at the thought of her being gone. Now I was unemployed and back on drugs. Without my grandma's guidance I was lost. So I did what I did best. Moved forward anticipating, that things between me and my lover would be different. That outcome would be a phenomenal happy ending.

His missed court date, added to the paranoia that the drugs already caused. It was very trying to deal with him at a normal capacity. But I did my very best. I still had to manage my own life and tie up loose ends. I put the jack rabbit on pause and the rest of my life as well. Fighting to get my job back was a lost cause. As they put it *I was quite the super star, climbing my way up the corporate ladder and the change I represented had no place in the corporate atmosphere.* Which really meant; *we know you are on drugs and you need help.* This had become a song that I was all too familiar with. Of course my lover was happy. I had a nice

Tamekia Nicole

sum of money, plus and adequate amount saved up. My grandma had taught me well and I was foreseeing everything going down the drain.

Living with my Uncle as head of the household was much different than living with my grandma. There wasn't much nurturing. There was love, but he did not play any games with me. I was grown but yet I was acting like a child. The drugs really changed my personality and enticed me to be shady. My lover enticed me to be shady. So I was shady. I was never quite sure of when my lover would be returning back to Las Vegas, and honestly I was hoping that it would be soon. I needed to get back on my grind and make things happen in my life. I couldn't just fall off AGAIN. I started sneaking my lover in the house every night after everyone else went to sleep. That was the hardest thing, to cut off my life, and cater to his needs and wants. I was truly loyal to him. Too loyal.

At that time, I'm almost positive my Uncle started to be suspicious. I was barely home because I had to entertain him all day when I was supposed to be at work. Sharing my newest unemployed status wasn't at the top of my to-do list. So I kept quiet. Direct eye contact with people was impossible for me because I wasn't myself. Smoking crack had turned me into a counterpart of the Devil. I had such a shameful existence I stopped looking at my reflection because I didn't even recognize myself. I hated what I seen. Friendships were once again in disarray and my tunnel vision only had him on the radar. Sneaking my lover in and out of a house full of people was a very hard job. He decided to not go back to Vegas until I had agreed to go with him. Fuck. Why did my life consist of the hardest decisions? I would not agree to go with him. I secretly wanted him to leave. So in an attempt to tell him that, I have to get back to my life. We decided to get a hotel room and have a romantic evening. That actually involved eating. When you are on drugs, you never eat. We never ate. We would ride around town looking for the next thing that would keep us high.

Whether it be easy come ups or spending all my money. The night at the room I told him, I can't do this same stupid shit like before. That he needed to go back to Vegas and I needed to find another job. My lover never cared about situations that could make me better or benefit us. He only cared about situations where he could come up. He was selfish as fuck. In the wee hours before we were set to check out. I had several missed calls on my cell phone from my Uncle. I knew this couldn't be good.

When I dialed him back, he told me to get out and I could only pick up all my stuff after I paid the balance on my rent. This was $500. That I had already smoked up. Fuck...I just said a simple ok and got off the phone. I looked at my lover for a solution. His face was blank. So I turned over and started crying. What would it take for me to realize that nothing good could ever come to me, if I am with him or around him? At this point, probably only death would wake me up. I was kicked out of my house, with a monkey on my back...two monkeys, if you counted him and the drugs.

At first the game plan was to just take the last bit of money we had and drive my car to Vegas to start a new life there. Drug free. That last part was hilarious. It sounded good though. But realistically there was not that much money between the two of us. I am the only one who had money. He was no help at all, financially or otherwise. But we would make it work by any means...that was our history. So because I did not have my $500 in rent, there would be no need to go to my house. With no plan and nowhere to go, he decided that we should get high. Of course we should get high. Wasn't shit else to do. So we got in my little convertible and went to the nearest spot to get drugs. Deep East Oakland. During those car rides I would be sick, because my body needed drugs. I would start to dry heave, pass gas and be close to vomiting. You would think I was on Heroine instead of smoking Crack. Sitting in the car was hard. I would fidget, look around. The wait was killing me. These were drug dealers that we were dealing with. We didn't call. We just showed up. Sometimes they were out of drugs. Sometimes we had to go to other dealers that we didn't know. Sometimes shit was just all bad. When things were all bad I would be sick and he would be irritable, but we managed to get thru it.

I became very accustomed to drinking 211's with a straw and any other malt liquor, to get a guaranteed buzz. We were able to stay in rooms for the 1st few weeks I was kicked out of my house. But we didn't really talk too much about Vegas. That was all bullshit, and we both knew it. We did talk though. We talked about us and how in love we were. This was nice but I needed to know what we were going to do. With the money running out fast and I was scared. I had been out of my house for almost

Tamekia Nicole

three weeks. Time was ticking yet I wasn't moving. Praying and praying for a miracle we sat in my car, smoking our lives away. It was so smoky and cloudy that we never even seen Fremont Police pull up on us. Really? The police? We were surely going to jail. We were smoking drugs and there were plenty drugs in the car. It was about 11pm on a Friday night. They ran our names. I was good. My lover wasn't. He had a domestic violence case that was unresolved. He never completed his one year program. So they took him, and left me. I cried and begged the officer not to take him. My lover just gave me a look like...*shut up dummy*. So I shut up. I sulked in the car for a little while. Then I started looking for the drugs that we hid from the police so I could use them. I found them. Turned the engine on and sped out of that area.

I lit up the blunt and tried to figure out where I was going to sleep for the night. Without him by my side I had a world of options. Hopefully. So many bridges were burned, in such a short time. Who was going to let Tamekia the drug addict back in. I really had no idea, what I was going to do with myself or where I was supposed to be going. By the looks of my gas tank, I wouldn't be traveling very far. I had to think fast, but those damn drugs had my mind spinning and I was sweating buckets.

Sadly, I just drove around all night. High and paranoid. My final destination would be outside of Fremont jail, where they were holding my love. This was no way to live. The sun was already up and the rays from the sun where killing my eyes. Short days and long nights. I was lost with him and lost without him. Finally, after deciding to back out of the jail parking lot, is when he called. He asked me where I was. They were getting ready to transfer him to Santa Rita Jail and if I stayed in the jail parking lot. I would see his bus go by. Sure enough, I saw him. I honked like crazy, hoping he could either hear or see me. Unsure on how long they would keep him, he told me to wait by the phone. I knew that if I didn't follow those instructions, it would be hell to pay. Back to reality, I had no gas and just a few dollars to my name. What the fuck was I going to do?

I was going to survive and hopefully have a place to sleep come nightfall. My high had finally come down and I was exhausted. Mentally drained to be exact. So I put a few bucks in my bucket convertible, hoping I wouldn't run out of gas. Next stop would be granny's house. Granny was one of the few people that I had left. I had yet to burn a bridge with her. With sleep on my mind. I was hoping that Granny would have mercy

Tamekia Nicole

on my poor drugged out soul. Terrified, sweating and shaking…I knocked at the door. She let me in. I sat on the couch caught my breath and asked her if I could stay for a few days. I confessed that I wasn't doing too well. She said that she could tell. Her exact words were that I looked like death.

Granny told me to get out of my dirty clothes and go shower and dinner would be ready. I did as I was told. That shower was everything I needed at that moment. Cascading hot water…but not hot enough to wash away all my dirt. Fresh pajamas and a nice dinner. I slept for three days…straight. I woke up confused. But thankfully I woke up. With a clear head, maybe, just maybe I could make one right decision. That is all I needed to give me a running start to several right decisions. I had never slept that long. Granny probably thought that I was dead. Damn shame. I wondered if my love had tried to call me. Then just as it had always been… we were connected. He called. Telling me, that they would be releasing him at midnight and I better be there.

I needed coffee and food. To my surprise my car had been towed. Apparently three days was too long to be parked in an unauthorized area. Oh my God, I just let out a really loud scream. Stomping back in the house, I couldn't believe my life right now. As long as he was in my vicinity I was bound to lose. All I needed was a game plan to go and get him by midnight. Then he called again. Fuck. Fuck. Fuck. I was scared to even answer the phone. But I did. I told him the car was gone. But that I would still be there. He sighed in disbelief. And so did I. This could have been the perfect time to leave him and try to resurrect my life. But I remained loyal and stupid. I paced back and forth around the house while looking at the time. I needed a way to get to him and then I needed a place that we both could sleep at for the night. Granny had already bent by letting me in, but she would not break… So instead I asked her if I could borrow $20 to go to the store. Reluctantly, she gave it to me. I kissed her and said that I would be right back. She didn't see me for five years.

CHAPTER 26

TRANSIETS

Love Made Me Do It

Tamekia Nicole

Without a car, Santa Rita felt like a million miles away. I took the light rail, and three buses and I was there just as he was putting the laces back in his shoes. I hugged and kissed him. Defeated by disbelief he suggested that we go hit some spots and try and get some shit to sell. I was down for whatever. Plus I felt like I fucked up since the car was now towed. Guilt was a steady friend of mine, he made sure of that. Getting high was the number one priority. That is exactly why we didn't have shit. With no regards to granny and going back there, I walked miles with him that night stealing anything from any store that looked like it could liquidate to either drugs or cash. We would take either. With four or five bottles of Patron in tow we landed in the projects of deep East Oakland. Patron was like gold out there. In exchange we had enough dope to have a decent night and enough money to get a room for the night.

The buses had stopped running so we walked miles to get that room. Only to find out that neither one of us could find our I.D. I begged the lady at the front desk to just let us stay for the night. She did. We blazed and we slept well past check out time. No shower, no getting ready, just getting out and on to whatever hustle would get us through yet another night. We were homeless, we were transients. Just not that dirty. Yet. No game plan. No need for one. We had each other and that would be enough. It would have to be. We started the day, by getting a lot of items to sell. Backpacks full of top shelf liquor, on both our backs. We walked from Central Fremont to Fremont Bart Station. Those backpacks had to weigh at least 20lbs or more. There was no complaining and barely any talking. I followed his lead. I wanted him and I wanted to do drugs with him. So I did as I was told. I walked miles with him. Unloading our back packs full of goodies... One city at a time. *Lord, please* have mercy on our poor wretched souls. We never talked about the fact that we were living on the streets with no clothes and barely enough money to have a roof over our head. Every day there was a hustle, there were no days off.

The clothes we had on our backs were the "fit" for the day, and that day only. We threw away so many nice things...you probably

Tamekia Nicole

wouldn't even know that we were homeless. We went wherever we wanted, picked out a new "fit", tucked that shit and left. We were the same way with food, we would go somewhere like a deli and eat for free. Very disrespectful behavior. Just like a couple of savage beasts.

Even though there were no days off, we did do things in between or daily hustles... like sneak into the movies or go have a beer and watch football. We walked to the Islander Motel from Fremont Bart Station, when we had enough money to get a room. They never tripped and it was the same price every time. The motel was actually housing for parolees and people on probation. It was a shady establishment for sure. The days were short and getting cold. We were slowly but surely running out of places to steal from. Times were getting tougher. But no matter what there were always drugs. Sometimes, I felt like they magically appeared. I would be so exhausted from walking miles thru cities...I was delirious. I just did as I was told and tried not to get the shit beat out of me. This was my real life and I felt stuck.

You could tell that all of the spots that we were stealing from were getting a little hot, but he never listened. I could beg and plead, really be scared and he never gave a fuck. Raleigh's Market. Not a good choice. Patron was behind the counter in an unauthorized area. Yet, he wouldn't listen. Fremont Jail is where we slept that night. I remember calling my mom from my jail cell. She was in Hawaii. She applied tough love and told me that's what I get. Tears swelled in my eyes, but I couldn't let them drop. In environments that are foreign to you, you should never appear weak. They will eat you alive. There were women that were accustomed to that life style. I wasn't one of them.

I stayed in jail over-night, he stayed a day longer. I just walked all night until they released him from jail. I was loyal to him. I was loyal to the hustle. I was loyal to the drugs. Sometimes he would thank me and tell me that he loved me, but mostly only if I said it first. This was a very rough existence, for both of us. I will never know his reason behind the decade of pain. It couldn't be that he loved me. I'll never agree to that. Going to jail didn't stop us, it only slowed us down. We had to figure out new spots to attack since our old ones were hot. I swear to God I wished that a job would just fall into my lap. But we all know that jobs

Tamekia Nicole

don't fall out of the sky, especially when you already burned up so many good ones. I just needed a way out. But the addiction to the drugs would not allow it. I was stuck in a jet that was shooting me thru all the phases of drug addiction. Soon there would be no chance for me. I would crash and burn. You could feel the fall breeze winding down the summer in all parts of the Bay Area. The seasons were changing and hopefully some positivity was headed our way. Even though we were robbing businesses blind, I was still praying for a silver lining. I don't know what or if he was praying for anything. It's amazing how you can think you know a person, but not know them at all. That was my dilemma. Poor judge of character.

Me and my lover kept on with what we had to do. The drugs were, wherever we were. We rolled blunts in public parks, fast food bathrooms, ravine's, buses....Nowhere was off limits. Every thought in my head was based around how to get high, how to keep my high, and how not to blow my high. Paranoia had started to kick in. I was so busy worrying about the Police, the Motel Managers, and the Devil. It was hard to enjoy anything, even sex. "I DON'T WANT TO FUCK YOU!" That's what I was yelling in my head. I wish he could have read my mind, since my mouth couldn't open up.

I remember us rolling a blunt in Arroyo Park in East Oakland. Scariest shit ever. First of all you are in the hood. Not any fake ass hood either. Being black and from the Bay Area you could easily see someone that you know. I used to be terrified that someone would see me like that. Although people knew that something was up with me...I didn't need the extra bullshit on my plate. My plate was pretty damn full. Arroyo Park was scary at night time. You were likely to see or hear anything. From... pit-bulls mangling passers in the night, to police chases, to people having sex. The worst was the pit-bulls. A pack of them would make you shit your pants. Imagine sitting in a dugout smoking dope and five pit-bulls run past you. They pause and sniff and look at each other. You don't move one muscle. You don't even breathe. That was us. High off dope, in a dugout...that had a big ass hole in the gate. There were many nights with wild animal encounters. We were stupid. We broke into Oakland Zoo and had sex. The animals were real. We heard them and I pushed him off of me because I was too paranoid

Tamekia Nicole

about a Lion that could potentially eat us. While reminding him that we could go to jail for being in here.

Sometimes I wanted to go to jail. I wanted to eat three meals, be warm, watch TV, and have some random girl grease my scalp. That's what happened in jail. I needed a healthier routine than the one I was on. It was so much jail time. I don't even know if I can remember all the trips that we took. The nights that there wasn't enough money to get a room, we created places to sleep. We slept in an alley way in Fremont somewhere, on a couch that was by an apartment complex dumpster. That night we had stolen something from somewhere and the Police were looking for us. We could see them, coming for us. Every corner we turned, we either seen their tail lights or their headlights. That was a long night.

It was freezing and that couch was covered in ants, and who knows what else. But we had to sleep. So un-knowingly we took turns. While he slept, I was awake, looking around, wondering and terrified. The police never found us that night. God bless the lady who seen us from her balcony in San Leandro. She gave us a pillow, a cover, bottled water and gold fish crackers. That was a big help to a night that would be spent in a park. We slept hard on our shared pillow. Then the sprinklers happened. Then the big ass Labrador happened.

This was hard. I wanted to die and I wanted him to die with me. My soul was already dead. My morals and my morale were at a negative zero. We weren't lucky on those nights we were blessed. Even God still believed in us and kept us safe. The motels were just as bad as the outdoors. People who were in situations just like you…looking for any way to keep the party going. To keep the high at a high. Motels were full of zombies, weirdoes, and druggies. We were no different. We fit right in. Sometimes we would walk so many miles my feet would be covered in dirt. My face and all other exposed body parts would be so dark from walking in the blazing sun for more than six hours a day. We slept in motel rooms that were rented at a discounted price because they had a foot of water in them, that wouldn't drain out. We took those rooms. We used drugs in those rooms. We fought like drunken sailors in those rooms. Time was still moving and we were still living. Barely. Once again the Islander Motel became a haven for us to have a safe keeping for the night. We broke a headboard one night, trying to do some kinky shit that I didn't even want to do. We had no manners. We just hoped that no one heard the mirror shatter as it slipped off the wall. He was always touching shit, doing too much. I did not want to be touched. My sex drive was at a zero.

There was the abandoned bus behind Union City Bart Station that he figured out how to open. My lover was a modern day MacGyver and an everyday asshole. But he was my asshole and I stood by him. I stayed in the struggle, and lost my mind. I was somewhere between heaven and hell. Purgatory. Sleeping on the bus happened more often than not. The bus was dark. The bus was gloomy. The seats were hard as a rock and the wind whistled thru the cracks in the door. Falling asleep was easy; staying asleep was the hard part. We smoked on the bus; we tried to fuck on the bus. He hit me in the head with a bottle of Bombay Sapphire on that bus. I remember the sun coming in hot and bright when we slept to long on that bus. It's amazing what you can do to survive when you have to. Arroyo Park was a popular rest spot as well. "Look at them; they didn't pay their PG&E bill, fucking losers." That statement woke me up. That night we slept on metal bleachers. Embarrassed, we got up. We headed to the Coliseum Bart Station with no destination, but we knew we could sleep on the Bart with the other commuters. No one would bother us with our hoodies on. No one would recognize us. Hopefully.

Being homeless was hard. Being homeless was scary. We were homeless. Some ideas didn't work without money. I thought that we could sneak into Fremont Hospital and sleep in an empty hospital bed. That was a stupid idea. We tried church doorsteps. Not everything worked. Nights that hair brained ideas failed it was always my fault. Sometimes I would be left all night on the bus, in the motel room, or at the park and he would be gone all night, to get drugs. I worried. I paced. We didn't have cell phones. So I adapted the patience of a saint. I had no choice but to be patient, it was either that or get my ass beat. I would sit up all night and just wait for him and the drugs. Most nights when he went on these missions I would plot to leave. But I had nowhere to go where I felt wanted. I fucked that up.

CHAPTER 27

JAIL TIME

Tamekia Nicole

Jail had become a permanent fixture in what we had become. Dope fiends, always looking for the easiest way out. Never paying full price for anything, and then wondering why we were once again in a court room in front of a judge. The first time we went to jail together I was terrified. The second time we went to jail I seen it coming. But yet he didn't listen. He never listened to shit I said. We were hot and known. Pictures were posted of us. Bonnie and Clyde. We were running out of slick reasons to be in a store and never buying anything. We were robbing people of their lively hood. We were single handedly inflating prices in the stores. Lunardi's Supermarket, Burlingame, Ca. There are certain areas that no matter what, if you look different than the general population, it's suspicious. We were suspicious. Yet in still we went in and tried to steal as many things as possible. Nothing was off limits. So we put our backpacks in a nearby bush and I checked my hair in the reflection of a car window. Even though I was scared to death, there was no choice in the matter.

We went in, got what we came for. Every big bottle of top shelf liquor that we could manage to carry out...we make it out. Then I saw the police SUV. My lover grabbed my hand and told me to run. We ran with our fingers interlocked. I was in flip flops, ripped jeans and an Usher tank top. Running across El Camino Real like the crooks that we were... There was a center divide that had a small waist high fence. He went over. I got stuck. The hole in my jeans was caught on the fence. Our hands slipped apart. He kept running. I was caught. Two police cars blocked me. I dropped to my knees like I was told. With their guns drawn, they cuffed me. They were looking for him. They searched for him. Meanwhile I'm sitting in the back of a tight ass police car, with my head down.

This was no time to cry. But how could I remain calm, my lover had left me. He ran towards his own freedom, while mine was hindered. Then he came out of no-where with his hands up. They slid him in the back seat next to me. The few tears that did drop he told me to wipe them on his shirt. "Never let these white people see you cry." I dried my tears. They put us in holding tanks right next to each other. The doors had a one inch gap under the door. We touched fingers and talked all night. Like I said as long as we were together, nothing else mattered. The law didn't matter and whatever the judge said, that's what it would be.

Love Made Me Do It

Tamekia Nicole

Time would never turn back. My lover would always promise that he wouldn't let anything happen to me. However he forgot that he had absolutely no control over the police. Although I knew that promise couldn't be kept, I always blamed him when shit hit the fan. I lived by his word, even though it let me down more than 97% of the time. I was a true fool in love. In court we would stand side by side, and he would be gesturing for me to chin up. We didn't kill anyone, so we wouldn't be there forever. So I was supposed to just *ride the shit out*. I tried but I was always scared. The women in jail were different than me. I wasn't better, but I was definitely different. I never handled jail well. Shit who did? Sometimes I think he didn't mind. Maybe he was ready to get some sleep and three hot meals. I think deep down maybe he wanted to be better than what he was, at least that's the wish I kept in my heart. That mentality is what kept me by his side. We met people along the way that contributed to the hustle. We would make new connects in jail to sell our merchandise too. We would call them or swing by their spot with what we had, as soon as we were back on our feet.

We met D boys, and baby mamas that did business with us. They let us use their cars. Sleep in their houses. They gave us dope on a discount. They enabled us, they used us and we used them. It was a viscous cycle with no end in sight. We had just got out of Redwood City Jail. I did a week and he did a week a one day. I walked around all night, with no money, in an unfamiliar city. I met a group of young hippies that took me in. I was scared to go with a pack of strangers. But I needed to rest. I needed to wash up. I need to have a glass of water. There was so much that I needed. I walked with these hippies back to their apartment. I observed everything in their apartment. I was in need but I wasn't completely retarded. I wanted to live to see the morning and to see him when they let him out.

Tamekia Nicole

They fed me, gave me hella pairs of socks, a new back pack and two fresh new French braids in my nappy ass hair. In the morning I felt refreshed. I thanked them and I walked miles back to the Redwood City County Jail. He was sitting on a bench lacing his shoes up. Just as he looked up, he seen me...there he is...my baby. Thru thick, thin and jail I was going to rock with him. He knew it, I knew it, and perfect strangers knew it.

As much as I felt like we were cursed and I wanted out. I never took the steps to free myself from the demons that possessed me. As deep in as I was, I would need an exorcism to rid me of the devil. I still wasn't ready. I stopped calling my mom every time I was arrested. The only thing I was doing was breaking her heart and embarrassing everyone in my family. I wasn't looking for help, because I already had that laid out on the table. I never took the help. I was looking for ways to pacify the situation, applying band-aides to gunshot wounds. So we went in and out of jail at least 12 different times. It never got easier, but we did start getting longer sentences every time. The judge did not give a FUCK that we were homeless. I always steered clear of San Jose. There was no way I was going to do any dirt where I was from and where my family still lived.

CHAPTER 28

DOPE DEALERS

Tamekia Nicole

As an addict, you must always remember a dope dealer does not give one fuck about you. They give a fuck about a few things; how much dope are you going to buy, and what method would you be paying with. Dope dealers are not your friends. They talk about you when they see you walking up, and they dog the shit out of you when you walk away. That was a part of the lifestyle. We had so many dope dealers that we interacted with. Some of them were cool and some of them looked at me like I had no clothes on. Once again, I was in unfamiliar territory. I dealt with situations in the best way possible. Anything for drugs right? Anything to make him happy? Anything so that we could have a peaceful night...

We had a dope dealer out of East Palo Alto that let us stay at his house for days, and use his car. The only stipulation was that we kept the bottles of Patron running like tap water. We did our best to keep that dream alive. We slept in a house with other people that we never seen only heard. On a mattress that was on a tile floor. I remember seeing a trail of ants in that room. But once I got high I didn't care, there could have been roaches coming out of the cracks in the wall. I would have closed my eyes and enjoyed my high. We argued in that house, and he popped me good.

They made us leave the house, so we left with no-where to go. It was the middle of the night. With our back packs and one blanket, we passed out in a Marsh. A stinky, muddy Marsh, behind the Dumbarton Bridge. When I woke up there was duck footprints around us, an empty bottle of Whiskey and for some reason my vision was blurry. My left eye was swollen shut. My head throbbed and I was covered in mud. I discovered the damage done to my eye when I say my reflection in a Jack in the Box bathroom mirror. He acted like he didn't remember, then he laughed about it. I didn't say shit...I still needed my other eye, so I stayed quiet. The show always went on. My lover got me a pair of sunglasses and we got back to business. There were dope dealers that we tried to rob and failed. There were dope dealers that gave us credit, there were dope dealers that sold us bogus drugs and never gave our money back. There were dope dealers that got the shit checked out of them if they were too disrespectful.

Tamekia Nicole

Women dope dealers were the stingiest. They felt like they had something to prove. It was always wack when we had to deal with a woman. Bag was short, dope was stepped on a trillion times, and sometimes the dope was too wet to even smoke. These dope dealers were something else, but they were our world. The way of life that we had become accustomed to was wearing us out. It hurt my soul to look at my own reflections. We went to jail eight times, while being homeless. No one had heard from me. I was a hit or miss with my family and with my friends. That hurt and sometimes still does. I made everybody worry.

Everyone who knew me couldn't understand why I stayed and why I accepted this lifestyle. I never had enough heart to ask for help and tell them that drugs got me. That I was getting my ass beat so much that sometimes I can't even see or walk. I couldn't do that to the people that loved me. There were a lot of shady and grimey things that happened in this ten year period. Some things I never lived down and some relationships I have never been able to fully repair. I accept full responsibility and accept that there are moments that I fucked up forever. The weather was changing once again, it was getting colder and the nights were long. We wouldn't be able to go on like this for too much longer. We would surely die. I had plenty opportunities to kill myself and a few failed attempts. But I knew...I just knew that God had something so great planned for my life. That hope kept me alive. Commadore Motel. This night is the straw that broke the camel's back. We had hit a nice lick at Stanford Mall, and I we had new clothes for our move to Vegas. We were supposed to be there by my birthday November 3rd. He promised and I held him to that.

It was the last room that they had we lucked out because it was late. There would be no other options except to roam around all night and pray that we make it to the morning. I was hanging on to the glimmer of hope that God could fix our situation. We were settled in our room, looking at all of our new fancy Vegas clothes and talking about a new start away from our demons. I took a hot bath and he rolled us up a few blunts. We kissed and smoked. But my paranoia was so bad sex with me was literally impossible. I had hallucinations that were visual and auditory. I was scared of my own shadow. If he attempted to have sex with me I couldn't get into it. Sometimes he would look like the devil and my coochie would dry up. He would give up and go masturbate.

131

Love Made Me Do It

Tamekia Nicole

That night wasn't particularly out of the ordinary. We smoked and smoked and smoked even more. Normal for us. The guy two doors down was selling us good dope and that made it easy. No traveling involved. We ran out of blunts and the store was closed. No big deal, it's about 1am and we needed to sleep. Vegas was supposed to be tomorrow after our last hustle. Instead of shutting it down for the night, my lover was pissed and left the room. I didn't think anything of it. I changed into my pajamas and got into the bed. Shortly he came back with more dope, probably close to a quarter piece. I was terrified when I saw that. I started thinking that we couldn't possibly go to Vegas if we SMOKED all the fuckin' money.

He sat next to me on the bed and handed me a glass pipe. I looked at him with tears in my eyes and said "You know if we hit this, there is no coming back." He didn't even respond to my statement. Instead he told me that when he puts the rock on the pipe that I suck from the other end (that was cracked, black and dirty} as hard as I can and don't blow it out until he tells me. I went deaf, dumb and blind after that. I never felt anything so powerful. I never tasted anything that good. I was sprung. Apparently he knew how to smoke out of a pipe. My lover hit the pipe with ease. Then I remember sweat covering his face...when he blew out the smoke I think he blew out some of his soul with it. This went on the remainder of the night. I was shaking, looking over my shoulder and looking out of the windows. He thought bugs were crawling on him. Our minds were slowly seeping out of our heads just like the money was seeping out of our pockets. I couldn't deal with the noise, the sun that was rising, the neighbors arguing outside of our door. It was too much. Not to mention how fast my heart was beating and my nose started to drip blood. I went in the bathroom to try and pull myself together and I couldn't. I really tried too. Instead I sat in a bathtub filled with about four inches of water and tripped out.

When I finally came out of the bathroom...the dope man was in our room and it was close to check out time. The dope man and my lover were having a conversation at the table. Shaking my head in disbelief I started to get dressed. The next thing I seen was unbelievable. The receiver on the phone in our room had a bag of dope in it. I was weak. I was calling on God to give me strength to walk away. While I was putting on my shoes and putting stuff in my backpack, my lover and the dope man started arguing.

Tamekia Nicole

My lover wanted more dope….BUT there was no more money. Literally there was no more money, hundreds of dollars gone in hours. The dope man was willing to take anything…even me. I had, had enough, he wasn't touching me. My lover reached into his pants pocket and pulled out a nickel….5 cents and slid it across the table.

I was crying as I seen this transaction. The dope man in return reached into his baggie and gave my lover a crumb. My lover put this crumb in his pipe and smoked it. I walked out of the room and took off down the street. A few blocks down my lover caught up to me. I was embarrassed, silently praying for either death or a miracle. Neither prayer was answered. Instead I was promised by him that we would be on the greyhound that night on our way to Vegas. He made good by his word. We begged several bus drivers for free rides. Hoped gates at a few Bart Stations and he went into a supermarket. Taking everything that wasn't nailed down. Including the save the children jars by the check-out stands, that had Lou Rawls picture on them. We made close to $400 that night after he made a few phone calls. No more drugs that night, instead we walked through four cities to get to Oakland Greyhound Bus Station. We got on the bus two days before my birthday and our next stop would be Vegas.

CHAPTER 29

VEGAS

Tamekia Nicole

I can't really remember if I was happy or sad, but I was definitely tired. My body ached, my head throbbed, and my heart was broken along with my spirit. We got on the bus exhausted. I was silently praying that my life would soon get better. Failing, to realize at that time that, everything began and started with me. I had yet to take ownership in the debacle I called a relationship. It was more like a relation-shit. The bus ride was excruciatingly painful. There was so much chaos, noise, people and all of that was coupled with a bad come down from drugs. We were scheduled to be on that bus for 13 hours. For most of the ride my lover was sleep on my shoulder and I just peered out the window…Hoping to catch a glimpse of better times. Far off in the clouds I swear I saw God motioning me to come to him. But instead of praying and accepting his call. I closed my eyes too and tried to relax. When we both woke up we were in Baker, CA. I was starving, my stomach growled so hard that I had cramps. We had no money. Desperate times call for desperate measures. With his empty pockets, and my big purse we were sure to eat something. While the bus driver took a 15 minute break we went into Rite Aid and did what we did best. Make shit happen.

The dry salami, Ritz Crackers, and spray cheese stopped my stomach from feasting on its self. I had no idea what Vegas held in store for us but I just wanted to eat, shower, and rest in a comfortable, consistent matter. I drifted back to sleep and when I woke up we were in Vegas. It was nice to be away from the poverty. I was happy for the moment and I saw the look of relief in his eyes too. Maybe my dreams of dying would turn into dreams of living. We did our best to freshen up in the bathroom before we were picked up so we wouldn't look like the wrecks that we truly were. His older brother picked us up from the Greyhound station and instantly I recollected how he could not stand me. But I greeted him like I would greet my own brother. I hugged and kissed him on the cheek and thanked him for picking us up.

According to him and the rest of my lover's family I was the cause of his demise and his addiction's. How far from the truth they were without knowing. I was the prisoner, the sacrificial lamb and whatever else he made me become. That first night in Vegas was amazing, and I say amazing because we were enclosed in four walls of a house, not a hotel room and I was positive that the sprinklers wouldn't start spraying us. There would be no pit-bulls lurking to eat us alive. So yes, it was amazing. His sister in law cooked a meal that was full of comfort and gravy. I tried

Tamekia Nicole

not to inhale my food like I hadn't been eating...but truthfully I hadn't been. But I also knew that if I embarrassed him in any way, shape or form. I would be beat up and marked up. So I smiled in between bites, made sure my mouth was closed while I ate, made polite conversation and said please and thank you.

I had become the perfect robot. It was never my intention to be fake ...it was impossible to be genuine. But I did the best I could. It was received by his family just as I thought it would be. Not at all. I was ignored during the conversation. Talk was going over me, around me and did not include me. Which was okay, I was in their house, miles from home. I just wanted to go to sleep on a full stomach, thank God for keeping me safe and wake up with a more positive outlook on life. I hoped that wasn't too much to ask for. The futon in the living room was offered to us. I only wanted a shower and to put one of his tee shirts and dream until the sun came up.

That was the deepest sleep I had been in, in a very long time. I don't even recall having a dream that night. I just remember hearing the sounds of bacon popping and then the aroma hit my nose. Sitting straight up, I rubbed my eyes, adjusted my head scarf and watched my lover in the kitchen cooking. I came up behind him and wrapped my arms around his waist. He said good morning, and then he told me to put some clothes on. Shit. I forgot I only had on a tee shirt and panties. I didn't need any extra criticism or talk about my character. So I changed back into my dirty jeans, put my bra on and put his tee shirt back on. His sister in law came down stairs and immediately I knew that this would not work. Her aura sent off volumes of negativity. I said "Good morning" and she replied with the same. Her tone didn't match my friendly demeanor.

Oh well, I was ready to eat this smorgasbord of bacon, eggs, and potatoes. I didn't want to touch anything in a kitchen that was not mine. So I sat at the table and my lover served me, then his self. The sister in law stood back and looked in her refrigerator as if she was taking inventory. My lover looked at her then at me, and he shook his head. It was obvious that she thought we cooked up her food, but we didn't. Apparently while I was still sleep his brother took him to the grocery store, and he had pushed out a cart full of food.

Tamekia Nicole

We finished our meal in silence. I went and folded up the covers and set them off to the side, out of view of any visitors. Then I sat, until my lover cut the TV on. Although it was technically our first day, I had a feeling that shit would be hitting the fan soon.

The day dragged on, I watch my lover and his brother play video games most of the day. It was so hard to keep my eyes open. I was going to need more than just one good night's sleep. But I knew it would be considered disrespectful if I sprawled out on the futon, midday. So I stay up and just sat next to my lover while he enjoyed his time with his brother. I understood...plus his needs and wants were more important than my need for sleep. Fuck it, I couldn't take it anymore. I leaned back and shut my eyes. Man... did it feel good, I pushed every thought and worry out of my head and commenced to sleeping. Unfortunately it was a short lived cat nap I was awakened by yelling and screaming along with the sounds of shattered glass.

"Nobody said he was coming with EXTRA COMPANY!" Now I got it...I was the extra company, and I was not welcomed. But in reality she had no reason to dislike me. The sister in law was as sorry as they come and never did a legal thing in her life, including work. She had aliases and bogus names for the bogus life that she lived. Yet in still, she judged me like she was God. I started to jump up and check her but her husband was already doing that along with my lover. The shattered glass I heard was an ashtray that his brother had smashed with his hand. I was unwanted by my lover more than half of the time. Now I was unwanted by a woman who jumped on the bad wagon with others. Honestly my lover did badly without me. I on the other hand excelled at everything I touched when we were apart. With no time to explain that to an enraged bitch... I started gathering my belongings and placed them in my backpack. My whole life was now in a backpack. With our backpacks on our backs, and harsh words behind us we hopped in his brothers Benz and took off. Destination unknown. But anywhere by myself is where I wanted to be. But instead we pulled up to a business office complex and I was instructed to get out. I sighed in disbelief as I am recalling these events. Our new home until we made money would be inside of an office that his brother used to record music. I looked around. There was a vending machine. But we had no money. There was a small refrigerator. But we didn't take all those groceries with us. There was no shower. So I would have to take bird baths in the sink. There was no stove. But there was a microwave. The only thing left on the agenda, was for us to stock up on lighters...although it had been a few days with no talk or using of drugs....this situation was going to put us in that frame of mind, seeking an escape.

"Oh well," had become my new all-purpose statement. We were dropped off and left in the studio. There was a computer and we had a portable DVD player so I would find solace in that. For a few days we walked around our new neighborhood, exploring the shopping plazas and taking anything and everything our hearts desired. New shoes, clothes, food, books, movies, you name it we took it. Which was really hard work and very dangerous since we were on foot. But it was the same shit we did in the Bay Area the last few months. Different state, same hustle.

I loved getting new things, even though I had nowhere to wear it too. I wore my stolen clothes; back to the store I had stolen it from, just to get more stuff. In hindsight, we were pretty dumb and reckless. But something about being with him made me feels invisible. I half assed believed him when he would tell me that he would never ever let anything happen to me. .Watching movies, surfing the internet and going nowhere in fancy clothes, was starting to play out. Boredom hit and it hit us, in a way that would not be avoidable. Idle hands are surely the devils playground. We were ready to play. At least I was, and I knew him long enough to know that look of being a fiend. I saw it every time I was brave enough to look at my own reflection for more than 30 seconds. At this point I had been with my lover for four years, and I knew he had a trick up his sleeve to alleviate the pain we were both having from detoxing.

I never said one word; I never mentioned drugs for a few reasons. One I did not want to be the reason that we sunk deeper into our addiction, and I did not want to give his dysfunctional family any fuel to further BBQ me. So I stayed quiet and occupied my time with books I had stolen. I would go thru 300 page books in a day. I would read all day and night. That was my escape. Occasionally we found each other attractive and made love and talked. But our temperament was edgy. It was only a matter of time, before we either killed each other or put flame to a pipe.

Tamekia Nicole

I had no money, I had no way to get any money and I never inquired about his money. But low and behold he had money. It was probably about $100 or so. There would be days that he would leave me in the studio with my books and my snacks and disappear on foot or with his brother. I didn't like being there by myself, stuck in an office with no windows, but I made do. One day he had been gone for at least three to four hours and when he came back he rushed to the bathroom. That right there was a tale-tell sign that he had drugs. The rush of knowing that you are going to get high is so intense that it turns your bowel system into an erupting volcano. Now that I had the notion in my head that we were going to get high, I dumped out my purse looking for a lighter that worked. I found one. Tucked it in my pocket and acted like I was so engrossed in my book just in case he wanted to act funny with me. See I couldn't act a certain way, or he would short my issue of the drugs or he would talk a bunch of unnecessary shit to me. So I played cool, until I heard the toilet flush...then I had a wave of nausea that almost knocked me out.

He came into the room I was in and handed me two little bags of dope and a blunt. I almost passed out. I was so happy to see these little baggies and a blunt. I immediately found scissors and started putting together my smoke able vacation. He disappeared into some other room and put on a porno. I heard in blaring so I closed the door and lay back on the sound proof foam that was our bed, and escaped everything. I had an out of body experience that night. I was relaxed, there was no paranoia and I felt the best I had felt since that first good night sleep we had.

My paranoia had become so bad that getting high was often more scary than fun. So I was relived to feel the actual high and not be hallucinating. We fucked that night, it wasn't love making because in reality we had no clue on how to love. Somewhere along the way we had lost that or maybe we never even had it. We just thought we did. The money he had made, doing who knows what, allowed us to stay high that whole night. He walked blocks and blocks to the ghetto, copped drugs and brought them back and we hit repeat. Spark up then, attempt to become one and experience orgasmic relief. It was back on,

Tamekia Nicole

and we were at an all-time dysfunctional high. He would push me around and cuss me out for not having money and having no job. Tell me I was ugly, worthless, stupid and a dope fiend. Imagine that. I had no job because I continuously allowed him to uproot me and invade my mind when I was doing well. I started yelling back at him. "I have no job because of you," "If I'm so ugly, what the fuck are you doing with me?" "I'm not stupid!" "I have no money because I have no job." Those words just echoed around the room…they never ignited him to think about his role in our situation. It was always me. It would always be me. So I shut up and locked myself in the bathroom and cried until I damn near threw up.

I was in a dictatorship. So the next day when we went out, I grabbed a paper and started looking for a job. I had no idea how I would get there but I need to have something of my own. Although he complained, he didn't want me to be anything better than what I was. I updated my resume. I circled a few ads, sent emails and made calls. But if we weren't there, I had no way of knowing if anyone called me back. If I did receive an email response, there were a million excuses of why I couldn't do something. I was truly stuck. I had to hustle with him, period. So I did.

We had new customers that would pick up merchandise from us at the studio. We also had dope dealers that made house calls. So I chilled and tried to stay in tune with his needs. My self-esteem was so low; my needs became null and void. Escaping those drugs seemed impossible. I mistakenly thought that if I followed him to Vegas that the drug use would cease, and that the addiction would just end. I was fighting a losing battle, simply, because I failed to be honest with myself. Time was passing me by and I was using drugs to pass the time. Without windows in that tiny office space I was never aware if the sun came up or even when it set. I was missing things that I had previously taken for granted. I'm not sure if my lover missed those small things or any other daily routine of sober living. I never asked. Every time there was a potential opportunity for us to talk about life, drugs were being given to me, or a pipe was being passed to me. I never knew how to say now. I only held out my hand, looked for a lighter and prepared for my out of body experience.

Days turned into weeks, weeks turned into over a month that we had been living at the studio. Occasionally, his mama would bring us a

Tamekia Nicole

real meal, or he would go by her house and bring back food for us. We weren't exactly welcomed there, maybe him but not me. We made do, we were no longer starving or cold but I was overdue for a long hot bath. Instead of a sink that I tried to fill up with shower gel and attempt to get clean. Right when I thought that he had taken the notion of making me, get money from strange men out of his mind…I had a rude awakening.

Unbelievable, but by now there were few things that could shock me in regards to the level of disrespect I subjected myself too. He had been gone all day with his brother and his brother's side chick. They all came in with smiles on their face like they shared a secret. I was told to get dressed, and refusing to move, I was knocked out of a chair and hit in the back with a beaded Mardi gras necklace. The brother and his side chick said nothing. Did nothing. I picked myself up and did as I was told. Locking myself in the bathroom I pulled my shirt off and examined my back. The same way I viewed all my battle wounds is the same way I wish I could see my brain and figure out what caused me to think so little of myself and allow others to treat me like shit. I was dropped off at Treasure Island Hotel on the Las Vegas strip with no instructions. Just a look, and that look was a look that could kill. His glare burned a permanent hole in my soul. I roamed around the hotel looking for a millionaire that would just want to talk all night. Instead, I picked up an old white cowboy that turned out to be an undercover police officer. I wasn't arrested but I was 86'd from that hotel.

My lover was watching from a distance, seen me get on the elevator and probably started spending money that did not exist. So when I came downstairs he held his hand out. I told him I was busted. There was no money and that I had to leave the property and he should walk away from me. Pissed was an understatement he was high and belligerent, shaking his head in disbelief he walked away. In the car with him, his brother, and the side chick, I was shamed like the two bit hoe; he was trying to turn me into.

Tamekia Nicole

I tried to sit back and ignore everyone, but my back was on fire from the welt that the beads left. I rested on my elbow and peered out the window and let the tears fall freely. I slept long and hard that night, fighting my drug cravings and fighting thoughts of killing myself. I woke up and opened the main door to the office suite and tried to figure out the time of day. It had to be at least noon. My lover was nowhere in sight. I didn't know if that was good or bad. The phone rang on the fax machine and it was his brother looking for him. "He's not here, no I don't know where he went, yup, and I tell him to call you." I hung up and wondered what now. He came sauntering in all sweaty and fidgety. He had drugs this I knew. I held my hand out to get my issue, and then I told him to call his brother. I vacated to my hideout… on the foam mattress with my lighter and my pipe. This is what life had become for me. I was once full of life, now my life was whatever was in my pipe.

My high was interrupted and short lived. Rent in the office suite had not been paid by his brother. We had to get out, right at that moment. They were coming with the Sheriff's and a padlock. I was in a fog, barely able to fathom the circumstance at hand. Now were homeless in Vegas too. What the fuck…Darting around every room, we gathered, picked up and threw away any and all things that looked suspicious. He was running around without a shirt with handfuls of our clothing throwing them into the back of his mama's truck. I followed suit.

Instead of going straight to his mama's house to return her truck, we drove around for hours and hours and hours. Smoking up everything including; our souls, pride and dignity. I was so paranoid and hot, I needed to get out of the car. Finally we pulled up in his mama's driveway and we got out. There were few words exchanged between me, him and her. She let us stay the night and we slept for almost two days. I was on the living room floor and he was in his mama's bed. I woke up before him and just watched him sleep. When he was sleep I could still see the attraction I once had. When he was awake, I could only see the Devil and a man that I once respected.

CHAPTER 30

IN LAWS

Tamekia Nicole

She didn't like me anymore than I cared for her. However, my heart was very forgiving and I was always willing to do anything necessary to mend broken fences. She wasn't that willing. This was fine. I needed to be able to shower, eat and be normal. I was in a constant dark tunnel, searching for normalcy with no flashlight. She agreed to let us stay, but in return we would have to get jobs and help with her 4 foster kids. I was in agreement with that plan. Now that I had an address and access to a car to get back and forth to work, I had action at getting back on at least one foot. My lover would not get a job; I knew that just as well as she did.

The brother was not happy when he received the report from the Office Suite Landlord. There was an extensive amount of drug paraphernalia left behind. I hated the fact that they acted like they did not know. I understand being embarrassed and in disbelief but they were as much of the problem as my lover was. They never said shit to him, they never addressed the issue. There was never an intervention only enabling. The brother tried to talk his mama out of letting me live there, I overheard their conversation and I started to shake thinking about where would I go, and how could I get back to my family. Luckily, their mama didn't put us out. I woke up early in the morning, got dressed, did my hair, cleaned up and asked her for the want ad section of the paper and if I could use the computer to apply for jobs. This was a good start for me. I let him sleep while I attempted to be the adult.

That following week I was hired at a time share company. They loved me immediately, I put up numbers, I hit every challenge and I brought home good checks. Half went to him and the other half went to his mama. Sometimes I would sneak and keep a few bucks so that I could buy lunch with my coworkers. Not only was I expected to go to work every day and give away all my money. I still had to be a part of what ever hustle he had going. I was so exhausted by the time I got off of work I didn't want to be a part of his scams. I did my part already. I got up and went to work every day, even if I had been up all night getting loaded. We had a few regular spots that we went to that were guaranteed money makers. Against my better judgment and following his orders, I spread the word to a few girls at work that we had the plug on shoes, clothes and baby items That was a huge mistake. That only cost me and made it awkward at my new job. One chick made an order of about $300 worth of stuff, but when the time came after work to exchange our goods for her cash…She played us, and gave us the run around. She insisted

Tamekia Nicole

that it would be good later on that night, and not to sell her stuff. Well later on that night came and went. There was no answer at first when my lover tried to call her, then her man jumped on the phone and it continued to go all bad.

When it was all said and done. I was the blame. I was at fault. So the next day I went to work with an eye so black, and bruised that blinking made me flinch in pain. When I saw my eye in the morning, I cringed at my own reflection. The foster kids questioned my battle wound. I lied and said that some cans fell on me in the pantry. They weren't that bright but between the four of them, they knew I was lying. I dismissed their questioning and continued getting ready for work. The drive to my job was solemn and filled with random noise from the DJ's on the radio station. I sat back with my shades on, thinking of what lie I could use at work. Unable to come up with one, I decided to recycle the one I used with the foster kids. I sat in my cubicle with my glasses still on, and just when I was ready to remove them. I was called into my manager's office. Not again. I would refuse to take another loss, I would beg for my job if I had too. Luckily I didn't have too.

When I took a seat in my manager's office I was asked to remove my glasses. I took them off and kept my head down. My manager told me I was beautiful and that I didn't deserve that type of treatment and I shouldn't be using that *stuff*. Looking at him in disbelief I played dumb. "What stuff?" Apparently the chick who played us, her dude is the one who my lover bought dope from 85% of the time. She told it all. I could have killed her. But instead I smiled at my boss, held back my tears and apologized for coming to work inappropriately and swore that it would never happen again. I never admitted to using any stuff, and dismissed his accusations of domestic violence. That was yet another mistake I made that really cost me down the line. I worked the remainder of my day, doing my best to keep the bruised side of my face away from my coworkers. But they knew.

Tamekia Nicole

It was so obvious. I had started my first day there and all my other days filled with so much charisma. I was bubbly and personable, but on that day. I was simply a shell of person. My lover picked me up from work and asked to look at my eye. I pulled off my glasses and let him look. Shame covered his face as he leaned over and kissed me. I smiled and pushed the incident out of mind. I put it on a conveyer belt in a box with all the other accidental, but purposeful ass whoopins. There were no more words exchanged. We shared a lighter, and we fueled up with dope.

We had many, many, fights either over drugs, money or both. That interfered with my work performance. To add to my issues, I had started another relationship as somewhat of an escape with a *woman* at my job. She loved me so much she was willing to buy me drugs if I just left him. I considered her proposition. I loved her in a way that was past intimacy. However I knew that he would kill both of us if he found out. I stay many nights at her house and used carpooling and saving money on gas as an excuse. I did my best to hide my feelings towards her but soon he discovered that something was fishy and when he found a letter from her hidden in the lining of my purse. All hell broke loose.

He was getting high in our bedroom and I was watching T.V in the family room after a long day of work. I had to wait to get high until his mama left for work. That wait seemed like an eternity. While I was waiting to sky rocket away from my problems he was looking thru my stuff. I was called into the bedroom and told to lie down. I did as I was told. He pulled out the letter and asked me to read it out loud, in the tone of voice I had written in. I kept thinking he was going to kill me. I read the letter out loud...the next thing I know is he grabbed my shorts by the belt loops and ripped them off my body. He delivered relentless amounts of blows to my body. I never saw such strength from him, it was terrifying. He yelled at me to stay quiet and not to move. I continued to lie still as he proceeded to examine my vagina. The woman I was involved with wore a lot of glitter eye-shadow. There was evidence all over my body. I was busted but I didn't care. He's lucky that I didn't leave his ass.

It was close to the time that his mom would be coming down stairs to leave for work. So he let me up with these careful instructions; "Don't

Tamekia Nicole

act funny, in front of mama." I knew he meant business. So I fixed his mama's plate and sat and made conversation with her. My body hurt, and I knew that he wasn't finished with me. As soon as the garage door closed he came charging at me like a raging bull. He slung me around like a rag doll.

He let go of me for a split second and I darted for the front door. Barefooted I ran for my life and as soon as I was literally an inch from my neighbors doorbell. He dragged me all the way back to the house by the hair at the top of my head *(hair still does not grow there.)* He beat me up half the night. I endured every blow and went to work yet again like nothing had happened. I never said anything to his mama she wouldn't be able to save me anyway. So I left my girlfriend alone and even though we worked together, I never even looked her way at work. His mama knew something was wrong, she always did. But she never involved herself in our domestic dysfunction. She continued to enable us and she probably secretly hoped that I never came to her with my problems.

Being high was our only escape from the fucked up reality we were in and his mama knew it. Yet we came in the house late with her car, with no apologies and just handed her the keys and locked ourselves in our room. She talked about us, but not really too us about the drug abuse. I feel like she could have helped but she opted out. Slowly we kept spinning out of control. The more money I made in commission at my job the more money was spent on drugs. However I also had my rent money for her. Meanwhile, he rarely was giving up his money unless it was for gas. I was able to treat myself and got my hair done. His mama made me feel guilty about that. So I gave her some money I had stashed so she too could get her hair done too. I tried to rectify every 10 shitty things I did in the world would at least one kind gesture. I wanted his mama to like me. I wanted her to love me like I loved her son, since I was feeling so disconnected from my own mama. I needed that connection and nurturing that only mama's could give. It was hard but eventually me and his mama we got to a happy place. There was no consistency to it, but I was content with the progress that had been made thus far.

Tamekia Nicole

Meanwhile the brother, the sister in law and the side chick all hated me. They stole from me, they talked about me behind my back and sometimes when I was in the room. I couldn't win. I had a job and money to support my habit, as far as I was concerned they could kiss my ass, twice. I stayed silent and found constant solace and peace of mind in drugs. Although I was in an okay space with his mama, I was still being used. I cooked, I cleaned, and I watched those bad ass foster kids. Plus, I listened to her rant about her lazy ass son. She always played devil's advocate. She would talk about him, yet never tell him shit. I would get random calls from his crazy ass sister in law, with wild accusations and arguments over pieces of junk mail that landed in her mailbox. When the brother would ride with us places, my lover made me sit in the back. The side chick only attempted to befriend me to get information about the wife. Everybody hated on me living there. But what I found out down the line; is that the brother, the wife, nor the side chick had any clue that I was putting in more than my fair share of work. Plus, I contributed an adequate amount of money towards household bills.

They never cared about how my days went, or how hard I tried and didn't care about the love that I had for each and every one of them. I just wanted to be accepted and feel good about myself and life again. Although they talked shit, and gossiped like old retirees they never had a problem with us selling or giving them stolen property. But they would gossip about how we were thieves. The brother tried to convince his mama to take the car privileges from us. I never seen such hate and dislike built up for a person they barely knew. Yet I dealt with it. At least I could escape Monday – Friday when I went to work. I had a talent for sales and my pay checks proved it. Even if I saw very little of my check, I knew that when I went to work…I worked. Although, I excelled at work and was loved there. I couldn't come home and start talking about my day. His mama worked a grave yard shift at a gas station, and tried to sleep all day and still care for her foster kids. While he either slept all day, stole all day, or got high all day. So my bubbly personality had no place, in a house that had very little happiness.

My lover would sometimes ask about my day, but when he did I was always suspicious. I had become so insecure it was hard to determine what was real and what wasn't. I was out of place in that house. I wanted it to feel like my home. But how could it? We slept in his mama's computer room on an air mattress. With constant reminders that we were two "over grown adults," that needed to get their shit together.

CHAPTER 31

CLARK COUNTY DETENTION CENTER

Tamekia Nicole

We never caught breaks, because we were not living right. I feel like we were single handedly robbing Vegas blind, and we were bound to get caught up. Things were okay with my lover. We had taken a hiatus from the drugs. But we hadn't taken a hiatus from stealing. I had become much more fearless than I was before. I liked nice things that were free. The rush that came along with breaking the law was unexplainable. I'm telling you, I didn't recognize myself. I was in contact with my family, here and there. Nothing too consistent. That was a void that I wanted my fucked up relationship to fix. Situations, where there was no accountability from the people involved could never be fixed. Simply, because you want them too, everything in life requires work, effort, honesty and accountability. At that time those characteristics were in my reach but I fell short, every time I relapsed.

We had a routine. He picked me up from work and we hit every store along the way home. Sometimes we had specific orders to feel to customers that were somewhat special. Otherwise you bought what we had or you just didn't get shit. There was no method to our madness. The goals were to get in, get out, and get paid. When we managed to accomplish those goals, everybody was happy. On good hustle days, we chilled, we gambled, we did regular couple stuff. That felt good. I was looking for love from him, and I had no idea how to give it to myself. Things were as they should be, because that is what I chose. That is what I prayed for, to be by his side. Instead of praying for guidance and will power, I was praying to be abused.

He was definitely a part of the nose dive I was taking in life. But I am well aware of the role I played in my own destruction. I had never given myself a chance to heal from my fiancé. I clung to the first sign of love. I confused game with being genuine. I confused sex with emotions. If the sex was good and consistent, it must be love. Or I used sex as a weapon to make men care. Never giving myself credit for anything besides, what a man needed me for. I enjoyed the normalcy that we were experiencing together. When we were happy together and others saw it, they couldn't help but laugh and joke with us. When we were laughing and joking that was a sign that we weren't using. When we were using, we never made eye contact when

Tamekia Nicole

we spoke. Shit, we didn't speak. Life off of drugs was nice. But we still had an addiction that we were battling, and that was the stealing.

It had become hard not to pick up things and put them in your purse, or your pocket. I never paid for anything. There was no need. I had built up a nice wardrobe, nice shoes, a few hand bags and I could eat out with my coworkers when I felt like it. I had hella money when we weren't using. He never wanted my money when we were clean, because when he hustled all day, he kept that money in his pocket. Instead of, stuffing it in a pipe. How long would this detox last though? That was the million dollar question. At that point I had seen it all. So I was skeptical, that all of sudden the drugs didn't matter. They were no longer in control of our lives...But I was in total support of us getting clean. I wanted to go to Heaven one day. I definitely wanted my own mother to be able to brag about her first born...Her only daughter.

A lot of unexpected stressful situations started happening to his family. Which trickled down to us, stress and detoxing from drugs will have an adverse effect every time. We weren't strong enough to carry anyone else's burdens, family or not. Getting out of bed every day, took a thousand deep breaths and positive thoughts. The first unexpected freak occurrence involved a fatality. There had been a robbery in the South West side of Vegas. A group of teens had broken into a neighbor's house. An altercation between two of them became heated, and one was shot point blank rage with a shot gun. There was suspect apprehended, and interrogated that denied any involvement. The suspect insisted that there was a masked man, that was also trying to rob the same exact house and he had killed the teen. The apprehended suspect was my lover's nephew by marriage. We were awakened by his mama, telling us to turn on the Channel 2 news. There was his nephew... Black as the night sitting in that box that sits next to the news anchor, as he tells the story. It was breaking news. I kind of cared. But his sister in law was faker than a three dollar bill. I didn't fuck with her or her shady ass kids. The nephew was her son .That was a serious situation. It was a pending homicide investigation. The stress and the talk about the case became overwhelming. His brother was there more than usual talking about the case with my lover. This cut into the time that we were learning to appreciate together doing simple shit. Like cuddling, & kissing. Now this crazy shit. So instead of being selfish with my lover, I supported him, supporting his brother in this dark time. I could feel the stress starting to consume us too though. It was like being in fog and as soon as the fog cleared. You accidently stepped in quick sand. Only one foot at first, so you still had action.

This was a test. How smart were we really? We managed to stay clean through the first round of trauma. I still had my job. I hadn't had any marks on me in a long time. Life was becoming manageable. The brother was in a sticky situation with his wife and his side chick. The side chick became pregnant and she was going to keep the baby. She was a punk bitch too. Ever since she watched me get hit with those beads and didn't say shit I barely said anything to her. I tried not to even look her way. She was trouble. That had been proven. As if there wasn't enough on our plate, the foster kids all 4 of them decided to blow the whistle on a few things…

His mama was whoopin those kids when they were out of line. By no means do I disagree with discipline. However I disagree with disciplining kids that are not biologically yours. Apparently those kids had enough of Nana, kickin their ass. So they told the agency. The agency came and took the kids from her custody. I was at work when all this took place. The only solution and choice we had, was to move out of that house ASAP. Before any law enforcement started lurking around, and asking questions. So we picked up and moved. It could have been easy, had we not been handed $500 cash to get all the necessary essentials to move. Had either me or him, been the least bit honest. We could have easily said that we are trying to remain clean, and with the revolving amount of recent stress….We cannot handle this money appropriately. It would be a cold day in hell before that type of honestly took place. So when we were supposed to be packing and moving while his mama worked the graveyard shift. We caved, and he blew the money. He blew every drop and I was an accessory. I helped him. I told him not to spend everything. We spent all night getting high and taking dozens of trips from the old house to the new house. Some of that money was supposed to be used for a moving company. That never happened, but you would have never known. We moved successfully without incident. The new house was a lease to own, and my name was on the lease along with his mama. I loved that house. It

Tamekia Nicole

had two master suites. One upstairs and one downstairs it was spacious and gave all of us the needed privacy.

Then a house of three, turned into the house of four. The side chick had her baby about three months prior to our big move. A pretty little baby girl, she died one day while I was at work. Apparently her grandparents fed her food that she wasn't old enough to eat. That was a sad day. That was a sad funeral and no matter how I felt about the side chick. I gave her endless emotional support. She lost her job soon after her baby passed, so in turn she lost her apartment. She was severely depressed. As I recall these times, I can still see her face and remember her difficulty and excruciating cries out at the baby's funeral. This was hard, I felt for her. I wished that I could have carried some of her pain.

She buried her baby and soon after that I buried my father. It was a long time coming. Still very shocking but expected none the less. My heart was already broken, because of the rift my relationship caused with me and my parents. I attended the services, but almost didn't because they did not want my lover to accompany me. I was defiant and defensive when it came to him. I paid my last respects and went back to Las Vegas .I was stressed the fuck out. Drugs were once again prevalent in our lives. So we used, to ease the pain we held inside, and we used a little extra to ease the pain that others transferred to us.

It was hard to use with the side chick there. She needed comfort, she needed eye contact. She needed humans to interact with. Since she was the side chick, the brother came and seen her when he could get away from the wife. Sometimes that was a long wait; I was expected to entertain her. While my lover locked his self in the bedroom using drugs. I was a horrible host. Night after night we went out after I came home from work and hit licks. There was a popular spot that generated a nice cash flow for us, that I was weary of going in. But he was so insistent. I followed behind him. I had left my purse in the car on purpose. I would not be taking shit out of there. It was All Star weekend and we had intended to make this quick money and go hang out. An altercation started between him and the store employees in the parking lot. I stood near the truck, being mindful of

Tamekia Nicole

covering the plates. My lover socked the store manager in the jaw, who thought he had a chance.

Weeks went by and the side chick began to feel better and cry a little less. Our routine hadn't changed. But I wish it had. That night we were sold some fake dope. My lover noticed right away and was going to go back to the spot and see if he could re-up for free. I rode with him. I rode with him two more times for a total of three times. On that third trip back home, we were racing against the clock. We needed to give him mama the truck so she could go to work. There was a high speed chase behind us. So my lover pulled over to the side of the road to let them pass. Only they didn't want to pass us, they wanted US. Our names were announced on the megaphone. We were directed to stop the car, get down on the ground and stay there. We did as we were told. The way they held us at gun point, I was sure that they had the wrong people. They acted as if we killed someone.

They took us to jail. We drove down the older end of the Las Vegas strip and booked into Clark County Detention Center. When I was searched I had a little less than a gram of cocaine on me. We sat in the booking room for hours. That night I learned out to sleep sitting up, with cuffs on. This shit was unbelievable. I and my lover were sitting a few rows away from one another and when we weren't nodding off out of exhaustion. We communicated with each other. He told me that when it was time to use the phone…Call the side chick and asked her to clean up our room. Anything and all items that looked suspicious, ask her to bag it up and throw it in the garbage outside. She said she would. Okay that was taken care of. Now I need get my charges and figure out how to get out of jail. I had to go to work on Monday. It was a Friday night in a 24hour town. A judge was not going to hear our cases until Monday, if we were lucky. I spent more than 24 hours in a holding tank with more than 30 women. There was a TV mounted to the wall, one toilet and one phone. I found a spot on one of the benches. Curled up, tucked my arms inside of my shirt and went to sleep. I only woke up because it was chow time.

I stayed in jail for 11 days. I was charged with a gross misdemeanor and possession of a controlled substance, and sentenced to a one year outpatient rehab program. They let me out at 7 in the morning. The first thing I did was call my job. I was fired. I inquired about my last check and they said it had been ready for days. I called our house hoping that his mama would answer the phone, but the number was either disconnected or changed.

I freshened up in the bathroom in the lobby of the police station trying to figure out a way to get to my job. As my co-defendant he would be getting out within just a few hours. So I waited for hours, and hours. I checked in with the Deputy who insisted that they were just a little behind. My lover never appeared because he had a warrant in the City Jail, which was another jurisdiction in Vegas. They had transferred him hours ago and he would be spending at least two weeks there. I felt weak. I had a few dollars in my pocket and I had planned on eating with that money and making phone calls. Now I needed to figure out what I was going to do. So I started walking and thinking. Cell phones had everyone so spoiled. There were few numbers that I actually knew by heart. Calling my mom was out of the question or my sister, those bridges weren't burned. But they were definitely under construction.

Tired and dusty I picked up the pay phone in front of the Greyhound station. I dialed his brother's number at first he didn't answer. When he finally picked up I told him the situation, and he said he would be on his way. On his way turned out to be four hours later. When I got in the car I didn't say shit. Options were non-existent at this point. I did ask about his mama, if she moved or was the phone disconnected. He basically told me that his mother wasn't fuckin with us, the police had towed her truck and there was drug paraphernalia found in the car. It wasn't that I was speechless, but I knew there was nothing to be said. I believed what he said, because it was the truth. That night that we were arrested we had been on a mission all day, more than eight hours. I stayed at his brother's house for over two weeks. He ended up with more than half of my last paycheck. Those two weeks were miserable. I was thankful but miserable. Their family structure was not set up for me. I wore his niece's clothes because I could not get to mine His brother and his wife complained about that. Damned if I do and damned if I don't.

Every time they went to the store I prayed they wouldn't ask me for any money. This situation was depleting my pockets. His mama finally took a call from me after I asked the brother to contact her. She was dry and unforgiving. So I let it go. My lover would be out in just a few days. I could hang on until then, there was no other choice.

Tamekia Nicole

Living in a house where more than four people don't like you is rough. I felt like I better wake up the earliest, eat the least, and be as quiet as possible in order not to argue with anyone. I am way too clumsy to be that careful. So there were snide remarks made on both ends, but mostly with his nieces. His nieces acted more like grown women than little kids. Their parents allowed them to be that way. So if they were smart mouthed with me, I let their asses have it.

The wife was okay, but you couldn't really trust her either. She was a shit disturber. She made up situations that never happened. You never knew when she would strike either. Her son's wife was alright we wound up getting very close down the line. Sometimes we would all hang-out. While my lover was still locked up I was invited to go have a drink. So I went. We all of dreams of getting married to our lovers, we joked about who would get married first. I always thought me and my lover would get married. I ended up with a tattoo that night of my lover's name. Big and Bold. Finally, the day came that he would be getting out and I couldn't wait to let him discover his name branded on me. I couldn't wait to tell him to take me home. I couldn't wait to be in our bed together. There were millions of reasons why I was so happy.

But when he came home he was already drunk, out of control and talking loud. He wouldn't listen to what I had to say. He kept touching me and pinching me. I was immediately turned off. This caused a fight. There were signs everywhere for me to leave him. I ignored them. I ignored all the possibilities of getting my life back. That first night he was back was uncomfortable and very similar to a roasting session with me and the guest of honor. They were a nasty bitter bunch of people. After a few days the situation with his mama was resolved. Upon my return to my house, I discovered that all of my clothes and shoes had been taken, by his bothers side chick. My father's obituary was gone along with all the pictures from the funeral. My check stubs and other personal papers had been ransacked. They were no good, but they couldn't blame it on drugs. They were just mean. Worrying about his mama and my missing items were the least of my problems. I was appointed to be in a rehab Mon – Friday for the next four weeks, starting the following week. This rehab was almost 30 miles from our house and with no gas and no job. I would be lucky if I made it to one meeting.

Tamekia Nicole

Although we were fresh out of jail, the criminal in us wasn't dead. It was simply resting until a desperate situation present itself. Drugs were a desperation situation they called our names like roosters waking up the world...when you heard the crow, it was loud and consistent, and it made you move. Everybody was watching us and everybody kept popping up. I tried to stay busy. I looked for a job. When I was high I just stayed in my room. There was no need to make conversation with people that came over. They didn't really like me anyway. Being high was the ultimate escape, but I could never escape all the trouble I was in. Now I had a criminal record in Vegas. Life was going to be hard for me until I decided I was sick of what was going on.

My last hope was going to be rehab. God please grant me the strength to get clean and stay clean.

CHAPTER 32

REHAB

Tamekia Nicole

07C232327

**DISTRICT COURT
CLARK COUNTY, NEVADA**

Criminal Drug Court Petition	COURT MINUTES	April 25, 2007

07C232327   In the Matter of the Petition Of Tamekia N Johnson

April 25, 2007	1:00 PM	First Appearance Drug Court	FIRST APPEARANCE DTP Court Clerk: Elaine York Heard By: Jack Lehman

HEARD BY: COURTROOM:

COURT CLERK:

RECORDER:

REPORTER:

**PARTIES
PRESENT:**

DeJulio, Douglas P.	Attorney
Johnson, Tamekia N	Petitioner
Porterfield Jr, Owen W.	Attorney
Public Defender	Attorney

JOURNAL ENTRIES

- Mr. DeJulio stated enrollment is based on a Conspiracy to Commit Burglary charge and an Attempt Possession of Controlled Substance charge (Felony/Gross Misdemeanor)in case C231382 with an arrest date of 2/24/07, and the Drug Treatment Program is an anticipated condition of probation when sentenced on 5/30. UPON COURT'S INQUIRY, Petitioner stated she is not living with anyone that uses drugs and is currently not employed but has experience in customer service. COURT ORDERED, Petitioner ASSESSED $10 per week, and matter CONTINUED.
5/02/07 1:00 PM STATUS CHECK - DTP

PRINT DATE:	02/11/2011	Page 1 of 6	Minutes Date:	April 25, 2007

(Actual, court documentation)

Usually I was the one to get the lighter sentence, but this time I was the only one sentenced to the rehab program. I was the only one that was caught with drugs. Living in a house with someone who wants to get high 24/7 is rough. Sobriety was going to be impossible. Maybe it could have been simpler if I really wanted to quit and he would stop with me. But once again I covered for my lover. I told the court that there was no one in my household who was using. Although I had justifiable reasons to why it may have been hard to shake my addiction, the judge would not care about any of those reasons. I was expected to be at the rehab and giving clean U.A's and participating in the program. Fuck. I had every intention

160

Tamekia Nicole

to get thru this. If I failed I would be sitting in Clark County Detention Center serving out my original sentence.

Rehab consisted of four phases. It was a year-long program. Every phase required giving urine samples. In the first phase you gave five samples a week, in the second phase, it three as well as in the third phase. When you reached the final phase, you only did 1 urine sample a week. The program was called Drug Court. If you were sentenced there by Judge Donald Mosely…you better complete it or you would be going to prison.

Rehab was very hard for me. It was hard to open up to perfect strangers. Especially, when you felt as if you had nothing in common with them. Giving a urine sample was a very belittling experience. There was a lady who sat in the stall with you. You could not sit down, and you pulled your clothes all the way down to your ankles. You collected your sample in the cup that they provided and handed it to her. Most of the time I found it difficult to pee in front of someone. But just like everything else in your life whether good or bad…you learn to deal with it. As much as I wanted to stay clean I just couldn't. I started getting worse. Although I was going to rehab, I had submitted seven consecutive dirty U.A's. The judge was going to have my ass. But I just couldn't shake the urge to get high. Without a support system and no will power it was impossible to stay on track, so I fell off. I stopped going to rehab and my focus was elsewhere. I was too busy trying to control a man who had shown me time and time again that there was no love between us. I submitted to him and everything that he wanted to do. Whether it was getting high or committing crimes I was in 100%.

Not long after I stopped going to rehab, there was a warrant issued for my arrest and I caught yet another burglary case. I was arrested and sent to jail. When I showed up in court, I was speechless. The judge ripped me a new asshole. This time when I looked over and saw my lover in court as my codefendant, I felt hopeless and stupid. He thought he had control of our situation. No one did, especially not him.

Tamekia Nicole

07C232327

DISTRICT COURT
CLARK COUNTY, NEVADA

Criminal Drug Court Petition   COURT MINUTES   July 24, 2007

07C232327   In the Matter of the Petition Of Tamekia N Johnson

July 24, 2007	10:00 AM	Bench Warrant Return - DTP	**BENCH WARRANT RETURN - DTP** Relief Clerk: Elaine York Heard By: Jack Lehman

HEARD BY: COURTROOM:

COURT CLERK:

RECORDER:

REPORTER:

PARTIES PRESENT:

DeJulio, Douglas P.	Attorney
Johnson, Tamekia N	Petitioner
Porterfield Jr, Owen W.	Attorney
Public Defender	Attorney

JOURNAL ENTRIES

- Mr. Porterfield stated the Petitioner is present and in custody and has been sentenced in the underlying criminal case and Drug Court is a condition of probation. Mr. DeJulio added the Petitioner is also held in an unrelated case with sentencing date of 8/20. COURT NOTED Petitioner has submitted seven dirty UAs and hasn't done anything in the Program. Court advised Petitioner that she owed $80 in fees. Colloquy between Court and the Drug Court Team regarding Petitioner being held by the criminal judge until the time of sentencing. COURT ORDERED, Petitioner RELEASED on her own recognizance, Petitioner to report to Choices IMMEDIATELY upon release, and ATTEND FIVE DAYS PER WEEK. Matter CONTINUED.
8/21/07 10:00 AM STATUS CHECK - DTP

(Actual, court documentation)

Tamekia Nicole

We stayed in jail the entire summer. I was miserable. I played cards, wrote letters and watched my surroundings. The only thing that kept my hope alive, was knowing that once I finished my sentence I would be welcomed back into the rehab. Although, I hadn't showed much promise when I first started, sitting in jail an entire summer had changed my tune. We wrote to each other at least three to four times a week. I felt as if our relationship may have a chance, now that we were dried up and apart. I always had the most mail that was covered in art and was at least five pages long. I lived for those letters. I wished that I could believe the promises that were expressed in those letters. But as I would soon discover those words, were just words on both ends. Broken promises and blurred lines. Getting out after a three month jail sentence made me feel brand new to the world, I just wanted to get in a nice hot bath and put on my own panties. You never know that things that you will miss the most until you no longer have access to them. Of course I wound up out of jail before he did, because we had different criminal backgrounds. So once again I would be calling to see which one of his family members could pick me up from jail.

This time my luck getting out of jail was worse than the time before. All of the numbers I had for his mama and his brother were disconnected. I got a ride to my house. Opened the front door with my key only to discover that the house I lived in was now occupied by someone else. The locks had not been changed. I began looking around to see if the owner was there, and dog started charging towards me. I slammed the door closed and started crying. On the way back to the car, I threw what used to be my house key in the garbage. I had been through worse and I would get through this too. Thankfully I had made a few friends in jail that let me stay with them, until I got on my feet. I only had the clothes on my back and I didn't know where to start. I wanted to sleep away my days and cry away my nights. But time waits for no one and I was no different. The best part about being in jail for 3 months was that I was clean & sober. I did not have any urges to use. I had a chance to change the direction my life was going in.

Tamekia Nicole

There was nothing more that I wanted than to be internally happy. There was a decision that needed to be made. I either was going to choose life or choose death. I was tired of other people making choices for me. The judge, my lover, his mama, his brother, and everyone else had a say in my destiny except for me. A whole month went by with no contact from my in laws or him. I carried on with my life. The clothes I had I washed those every other day and washed my panties and bra out every night. I borrowed money from my friend so that I could get on the bus every day and go to my rehab program. I was down but not defeated. I tried to hone in on what God wanted me to do. His guidance was drowned out by the other noise in my head, which I assume was the devil trying to lead me astray. Finally I heard from my lover. He was out and had moved in with his mama, his brother and his side chick. What a relief to know that he was okay. His clothes were carefully moved on to a new house, but my belongings could not be accounted for. This was life as I knew it. This was life as I allowed it to be.

I wanted to be mad, I wanted to fight about my clothes, shoes, and Lord knows I wanted to fight about my pictures and keep sakes…but why, when I had zero chance of winning. So I stayed silent and went with the flow of things. Rehab was going okay, I learned to open up to the groups I was in and take from the program only what was needed. I soul searched and made promises to God that I would do my best to keep. I prayed so hard and so long that tears would stream from my eyes. Something was bound to change. Not knowing what the change would be. I just kept moving forward on my own behalf.

Feelings of suicide came and went. Feelings of using came and went. But the feeling of being alone stayed with me. My loneliness sometimes came out during my group sessions in rehab as I fought back tears. Often people thought I wanted someone to feel sorry for me. That was never the case. I wanted someone to say that they understood and give me a fool proof plan. That not even I could fuck up. I was moving thru my phases in the rehab and I felt good. I had moved around a bit with a few different friends. Quickly I learned who was really down for me and who was trying to come up. I had made what

Tamekia Nicole

I thought was a good friend. But her and her god sister attempted to pimp me and thought I was going to be cleaning the house as payment for room and board. Guess what? I wasn't going to be participating in any of those plans. I was trying to do the right thing.

I finally settled in with someone who had enough room for me to be there as long as I needed, with no underlying motives, for me to bring in money or be a maid. That felt good. My lover had helped replenish my wardrobe. Finally an end to my same clothes every day marathon. The only major issue I had with my new roommate was.... she was a dope dealer. As a recovering addict with three months under my belt, this would be a true test of my will power. Lord, please help me keep my demons away.

CHAPTER 33

BATTLING DEMONS

Tamekia Nicole

My new roommate was very mindful of my situation. I was mindful that she needed a resource to make money. I stayed busy and when she was serving those in need of drugs, I distracted myself. By court order I could not live with my lover. I could only see him on weekends and that was perfect for me. I only needed him in small doses anyway. This worked well for us, because it gave us the opportunity to miss one another. Plus get our own lives together. I knew that if I was away from him, I could get a lot more things done for myself. I was blessed to get an awesome job. Slowly I started saving money and acting like an adult. Before I knew it I was promoted to Assistant Manager in the call center I was working for. At first it was rough the same group I started with, were now my employees. The hated me. I could care less. I was on a mission to find a level of success. I worked hard every day, went to rehab from work. I was at peace with myself. My probation officer was very proud of me and I had submitted nothing but clean U.A's for months now. My lover picked me up every Friday after work. We were doing what normal couples did. We made love, we went to the movies, we went to buffets and we truly started enjoying each other. The fact that we had the ability to reconnect after all the damage was astounding. I loved every moment that we shared together.

Of course every wonderful moment that I had involving him was short lived. We had decided to go out to breakfast one Saturday morning, me, him and his mama. That's when she asked me how I felt about his brother's side chick coming to work at my job. I was floored to say the least. I was unaware that she applied and was hired. Apparently I was the only one that didn't know. If you hated someone, stole their clothes, and did everything in your power to destroy them...why would you come and work where they worked? My only answer is... to further destroy their hard work. This is exactly what she tried to do. I was always the bigger person. I always welcomed everyone with open arms, even my enemy. On her first day of work, I walked over to her department and welcomed her to the company. I bought her lunch and made her feel at home. I was comfortable with whom I was, and the purpose I served within that company. I was special and the owners adored me. I was carefree and flourishing in my new position.

Tamekia Nicole

Upper management was well aware that on some days during the week, I left early to go to my rehab program. Not everyone I worked with knew this information because they didn't need it too. I was fighting my demons successfully or so I thought. One day out of the month I would go and see my Probation Officer and give reports of how I was doing. I was honest about my criminal past and my ongoing battle with drugs. But the side chick felt that it was necessary to tell anyone and everyone that did not know. That I was a drug addict. She was very bold, telling all my business in a break room when I wasn't even there to defend myself. She was a sneaky, ungrateful, hateful bitch. Those are harsh words and although I know longer feel like that. At that time she had shown me nothing to the contrary, to make me think otherwise.

When I found out what was said from a reliable source. I immediately contacted my lover. Luckily she never came back after that day. Neither my lover, nor his brothers were too happy about her actions. Idle chit chat like that in a corporate environment would stop the flow of money. No one could agree with that. This was one of the few times when my lover and my in-laws had my back. What a relief, had their not been anything done. I was going to make every day she worked a living nightmare. The drugs weren't much of an issue. If I felt triggered to use I talked about it, in my groups. I never worried my lover with how I felt, because I was being mindful of what may trigger him. The traffic at my house picked up. I noticed that addicts were frequently at the door or inside the house when I was there. I never said too much about it because I had no other options. Being homeless so many times really humbled my words and actions towards others. But deep down inside I knew that this would not be a safe place for me too much longer.

With the side chick gone, I was able to once again be carefree at work. The job was a lot of pressure, I had to make sure that I had a team that produced numbers and took care of customers the right way. Although I was apprehensive when I was advised that I would be getting help from a manager that the company was going to bring in...it gave me a sense of relief. I was looking forward to building an allegiance with a person that had more skillset than I did at being a manager.

Tamekia Nicole

Unnecessary stress could cause demise in my efforts at doing things the right way. Red flags immediately were raised when I met who they brought in. Trying my best not to be judgmental I welcomed the new manager with open arms. Showed him the ropes and educated him on our products and what our goals were. We hired a few new people together. One of my new hires was his brother's daughter in law. Under new management, with a "family member" in my department, I expected every day to be a cake walk. To some extent those minor changes made my stressful work days, much easier. I had someone to complain too and gossip with. My new manager was definitely on drugs, but as long as I did not let the effect my work performance I didn't care. I was there to work and get paid. I was not there to babysit or save the world. I was still trying to save myself and I was still so far away from that.

My rehab program taught me. That the first five years of becoming clean you must be selfish. You must change your people, places and things, if you wanted to successfully go from user to quitter. I lived by those words and still do. When it became too much to handle, I confided in the owner and let her know my concerns. She assured me that I was wrong, and I left it at that. Meanwhile I was noticing a change in my lover. I began having thoughts that he was once again cheating. So I began investigating. Since, we were not in the same household, except for on weekends. I started my investigations with our phone records. I was the main name on the account I had access to our records online. So one day on my lunch break, I looked at all his incoming and outgoing calls. There was a trend of bay area phone numbers. That I knew were not numbers of family members, so I dialed the ones that I saw the most.

My suspicions were right on the money. Tons of girls had been made tons of empty promises by my lover. This whole situation was running into the ground, just when I thought that things were getting better and we were conquering our demons…I was proved wrong. The stories I heard from these women shattered me. But honestly I was not surprised. Disappointed but not surprised. It was Friday and my lover would be arriving shortly to pick me up. That is when I would show him his phone bill; I had highlighted all the suspicious calls and the call duration. I was curious to see how he

Tamekia Nicole

would get out of this. I rode all the way to his house, like I had no issues. But I was boiling over inside.

When we got all settled in comfy and cozy I reached into my purse and pulled out exhibit A, my evidence that he was still a liar and a cheater. He was speechless as he half-heartedly looked at those phone bills. There was no explanation but there was a resolution. We needed a break from each other. I told him to figure out if I had a place in his life. Then I called my coworker to come and get me. There was no way that I was staying that weekend. Or any other weekend until the dynamic of our relationship was in a consistent happy place. I carried on with my life. Work, rehab and piecing together relationships with family and friends that suffered because of my addiction. It was hard work, and for some reason I thought it would be easier than it actually was. I was a no show for everything. When my friends came to town, I made promises to meet them or excuses as to why I couldn't be there. I wanted to be the person, that they remembered not the demons that consumed me. It was too complicated to explain over the phone. I would let me actions talk for me. Leaving him alone was my first step towards that goal.

Drugs were everywhere around me. They were in my home, they were at the rehab, and sometimes I seen people lighting crack pipes at the bus stop when I was on my way to work. It was like the more I tried to focus. The more vulnerable I became. I wanted to say and believe that life wasn't fair. But my results were in direct correlation with my previous actions. Work was okay. I had my in-law as my right hand man and that made work bearable. My new manager was getting stranger by the day. He was weird and paranoid. I watched him like a hawk when it was slow. He looked out of the blinds for no reason. Sweated profusely and was always confused. Tell-tale signs of a drug problem. Then one day right before a staff meeting. A back of cocaine fell out of his slack pocket. I knew it. I had no idea what to do with this information so I just waited and continued to watch him. Then just as I knew it would. The tables turned on me. I learned that when others consider you to be a threat they also watch, wait, and plot on you. He may have been on drugs but he was no dummy.

Tamekia Nicole

Much like sand in an hour glass, my time on top was coming to an end. I was too much of a threat. I was smart and since my brain was clouded by drugs. I was on my A game and everyone knew it. Every night I came home exhausted, frustrated and running out of ways to keep my mind from wondering to the depths of Hell. My roommate decided that her boyfriend should come and stay with us. Right then I knew that this situation would also be short lived. A man can always come between friends. Especially if that man is no good, he was no good. He had no job and no ambition. His plan was to live off of her hustle. I was steadfast in my separation from my lover. We talked but when we did it was dry. There was no life left in our relationship because it was built on a foundation of lies and no trust. We failed at being in tune with the other person's needs. I called out of habit and worry. It was a codependent situation. I never gave him enough breathing room to be a man and to show me something different. On this particular night, our phone call went way different then I could I could ever anticipate.

My lover had been feeling sick with a migraine so our conversation was short. I suggested that he take medicine and go to bed early. He called me the next day and said that he was going to the hospital. That alarmed me. Men hated Dr.'s and hospitals. So I knew that it was serious. Later that evening his brother's wife called and told me that my lover had suffered a massive heart attack. He was in an induced coma. My heart dropped out of my body and life as I knew it was upside down. My thoughts gravitated towards all our recent fighting and all the struggles that we had overcame. The thought of losing him made me drop to my knees. I went to work advised my manager of the situation. I spent the next three days by my lover's side in Intensive ICU.

Luckily he went to the hospital in time. Instead of cracking his chest open. They repaired his heart valves by going in through his groin. Three of his heart valves were clogged with Cocaine is exactly what the Dr. told me. I was shocked. All the lies about the other women and now come to find out...He was lying about being clean too. But no matter what I wanted him to get better. If I had to nurse him back to health I would. Drugs only caused death and destruction.

Tamekia Nicole

Everything I could have ever dreamed of was already destroyed. I begged God not to bring death to my door step. Those three days were hard for me. It was hard to see him in such a helpless state. It was unbearable to see him in so much pain. I would have done anything to take that pain away from him. Upon his release he was given specific orders to rest, and not use. Those instructions fell on deaf ears after a few months. Although it's not a valid reason or justification to use drugs, over stressed situations can push anyone over the edge. Soon I would be joining him my edge was closer than I thought.

With him constantly on my mind, everything else began to fade to black. Even though, I was still clean and sober. My mind thought about just getting a little bit high. I wanted to ease the pain that my heart couldn't manage on its own. I started watching my roommate very closely. Hoping to get a glimpse of where she kept her stash. One night she threw a party and while her, and her man where passed out. I ransacked the house looking for drugs. I crept in her room and looked thru her dresser drawers. When she moved I dropped to the floor and crawled out of there. I was turning back into who I was running from. The demons were calling me and I had no idea how I would silence their demands on me. I wanted God to end my life, but even he still had mercy on me. Living was agony, and I prayed that death would defeat me.

CHAPTER 34

ON THE RUN

Tamekia Nicole

My stresses began to triple. My urges were uncontrollable. It had been just a few months since he had his heart attack. Getting high became the subject of conversation. Money in large amounts was always a burden for us. We were supposed to be having a date night, but as soon as drugs became the topic. He made a U-turn to go and cop drugs. Fuck. I wanted to get high but I didn't want to be paranoid and think about the police or FBI kicking in our door. I didn't want to see the imaginary man with the flashlight. The rehab program and his heart attack were the least of my concerns.

I just wanted to get high and I would kill someone to make it happen, even if it was my self. When I lit that pipe, everything that was bad in my life was non-existent. Everything meaningful in my life took a back seat. Nothing and no one was more important. We went on a three day binge. I called in to work and skipped my rehab program for the day. I would deal with the repercussions later or not at all. It felt good to be high, similar to a first kiss. You're nervous but you know with each hit, it gets 100 times better. I was seeking long term gratification from my on again love affair, with Crack. Life spiraled, downhill fast. As soon as, I touched that pipe, I granted access to my demons. I started to lose everything. My roommate situation was the first to deteriorate. I was in the last phase of the rehab program. I had learned different techniques to make sure my urine was clean when I was tested. I knew I was buying time and not solving the problem.

Those techniques failed eventually...I came up dirty. My first dirty, in months. The judge cut me some slack, but advised me to report to my Probation Officer prior to returning to rehab. Too scared to report to my Probation Officer; I decided that I would never go back to the program. God didn't take me going back on my promise and prayers to lightly. Life at work took a twisted turn for the worst as well. Work life was already strained since my new manager started. I felt as if I was going to be fired, and I was. Although my in-law that I hired managed to stay employed. I was shown the door and given my last check. I saw it coming and I had no one to blame but myself. The only thing I thought about was rationing my money. Until, I found something else. I thought about telling my lover and his reaction. In the past telling him I had lost a job never went well. Being called stupid and worthless would send me into a rage. But I had to tell him, so I did. Right after I told him. His brother asked me if he could borrow $800 to buy a new car.

I was fuckin speechless. But none the less I was talked into loaning him the money. I never saw that money again, not even a portion of it. The next few days came and went it was almost like I was in a fog that wouldn't lift. I stayed undressed and in his bed. Plagued by my own dumb decisions, it was hard to fathom that I was once again on the wrong side of the law and back on drugs. Dealing with it the best way I knew how, I masked the pain with Cocaine. My existence in the world shrank with every hit. Maybe if I smoked enough I would just disappear into thin air. The relationships that I had formed with a few people came to a cease and desist. I knew it would only be a matter of time before I would have to permanently take cover because of the felony warrant that was attached to my name. Rehab was my last shot, and I blew it.

Days, nights and eventually weeks went by. I had barely moved, unless it was to look for a lighter. Somehow we were once again in the same household. I came over that night after I was fired and never left. The house we lived in was so crowded. Me, him, his mama, his brother, and the side chick and their new baby. In the midst of all the confusion there was yet another loss suffered. My sister in law, his brother's wife, had been in a terrible car accident. Two of her children were in the car with them along with one of her daughter's boyfriends, and a friend that had snuck out. On their way home from California, they hit a center divide. Everyone in the car died except for my sister in law. I was residing in chaos. They say *that chaos breeds chaos*.

While, everyone was dealing with their own tragic circumstances, I was trying to get my job back. To no avail I was still unemployed. They denied my unemployment benefits. So on top of everything else I would not have any income coming in. This was good for my lover, because now I could go back to being his Bonnie. I didn't want to be his Bonnie. My savings was dwindling down. His brother was ducking & dodging me. So, I had no choice. I emptied out my big purse to make room for stolen goods and we were back at it 3-5 times a week. It was no longer a game just to come up.

Tamekia Nicole

It was a survival technique. His mama was on me daily about getting a job, but never once said anything to her son. It was all on me. Every morning when she came home from her graveyard shift, she knocked on our door handing me the classified section of the newspaper.

Most of the time when she would be knocking at the door I had just fallen asleep. One morning I had plan on cussing her out because she was beating on the door so hard. When we didn't answer she came thru our bathroom door. Only this time she wasn't handing me a newspaper, she was advising us that she had seen our picture in a store as WANTED THIEVES. Terror was spread all over her face. Not so much mine or his. We had pictures of us in several stores. The only thing we cared about was which store and how clear the picture was. I generally wore hats and had learned to put my head down upon entering any store. We listened to her go on and then we went back to sleep. Since we were using her car we had to be extra careful as to not make her car hot. Its official we were the scum of the Earth. The quicker his family realized it, the better it would be for us. They were 100% enabling us.

I was tired of being on the run with no money. I started devising a plan to get back on my feet. I had to go back to work ASAP. I read up on Nevada state laws. Which stated that if you had a low level felony; which I did, and you stayed out of trouble for five years or more. When you were caught they would dismiss your case. Oh my God, thinking about being on the run for five years made me weak. If I kept up on the track I was on, in five years I would be dead. Thoughtless, reckless and wild…that best describes what we were. I was a passenger in two high speed chases and one close encounter with an undercover officer. Luckily my airtight alias allowed me to get away. Even though one encounter my lover had said my real name. It was as if he was tried to send me away. But God had me and I was let go. Pacing around one early morning with a list of job possibilities I decided to place a few calls. Bingo! I was called in for an interview and hired. It was a call center that needed sales reps. This was perfect because I definitely had the gift of gab. However I had no I.D, and I was a fugitive, so this would be a tremendous gamble. If the Probation Department ran my social security number and seen that I was working. I would be locked up.

Tamekia Nicole

That never happened. I worked and made new friends. I found myself once again handing over entire paychecks that raged from $400-$800 a week. I felt okay about myself. But it was hard to be happy, since I was hiding from the law. I had no one to confide in. The domestic abuse wasn't as bad, a push here, and a chokehold there. Those I could take. Flying fists I could not. For some strange reason, I always thought I had done something to deserve that sort of abuse. But in reality I hadn't done anything. Men who are insecure with their self will blame you for their own short comings. That's what he did. He showed up to pick me up from work drunk and unruly. He was an embarrassment, but he was mine and I would defend him until the end of time. I was also sick. I was brainwashed. Every day it was the same. I busted my ass trying to meet sales quotas and then I would be out all night hitting stores and scoring drugs with him.

Friday's were always happy days for me, this was pay day. On this particular pay day, I was feeling like I should just turn myself in and get away from this asshole. When he started talking shit, and insisting that I give him my whole check; I jumped out the car at a red light. Only to be dragged back. This was a hopeless situation. So I stayed and I took it. My hair had been grabbed so many times in the middle of my head that hair will barely even grow there. He stunted my growth as a person and he took away all my basic rights. Yet, he never owned up to anything. The lights & gas were cut off. I had a pocket full of money but there were three other grown people in the house. I felt no need to chip in. I was paying more than my share. So when they cut off our power we stayed in our room, with our flash lights and pipes. I prayed for death. But God never answered.

The lights being cut out, was just a prelude to being evicted. Apparently, the new car I helped his brother purchase took all of his brother's money. He collected $400-$500 a month from us as our portion of the rent and other household bills. He never once paid the landlord. So the Sherriff's put a pad lock on our front door. All this happened while I was at work busting my ass.

Tamekia Nicole

The best thing about Vegas was that there were always houses for rent. We found a beautiful five bedroom house. We were as whole, as one dysfunctional blended family could be. I continued to work as my escape from him and using. I formed a few close relationships with my coworkers. I found some peace in unleashing all the anguish I felt inside, on their shoulders. My lover's chest began to bother him more and more. It had to be the drugs that were causing him to be sicklier. Then one day, just like several times before. He decided that it was time for us to quit. We threw out all drug paraphernalia, onto the side of the freeway.

New start to an old life, I was fine with that. I had decided months prior that quitting was inevitable. But it was never my call. I even decided to try and be friends with his brother's side chick. I needed a friend in the house. I had reservations about befriending the side chick. She had been disloyal since day one. But I was going crazy in that house. So we hung out one night. Intending to go skating, but the skating rink was closed. We wound up drinking and gambling at the casino. *Loose lips sink ships.* Once the side chick consumed alcohol, she sure had a lot to say. She wanted to hurt me. I was unsure of her motive, when she confessed that she had something to tell me. "Can I tell you something and you won't say anything?" My reply was "Of course." I had not one intention on showing her any loyalty. But I had every intention to get information from her. She informed me that my in law that I hired had been sleeping with my man...For years, according to her. I was devastated and in complete shock. I listened as she described their supposed affair.

Immediately I text the in law, we had become very close over five years. I trusted her to an extent. She denied every accusation via text and when I came home to question my lover. I was slapped repeatedly every time I stood up I was slapped. Until, I stopped getting back up. Even his mama couldn't stop him from whaling on me. I cowered into the spare bedroom and stayed in there the whole night on a deflated air mattress and no pillow. I was being punished. When he asked me where I got that information I told him. The side chick denied everything. I wasn't the only one beat up that night. She sported a black eye. When I crossed paths with her the next morning, I laughed to myself. Although it was wrong, why did she lie, and more importantly *was* she lying?

I carried on. Now more cautious than ever, I was living in a house where everyone was conspiring to get me. No one in his family liked me,

Tamekia Nicole

and I couldn't trust any of them. There was so much disloyalty. I had no one to run too, but my coworkers. They were probably sick of me complaining about someone who was CLEARLY a loser. So I stayed quiet.

After the accusations I made, I also had a black eye. I went to work with a partially black eye and plotted to leave him. I plotted to make the most money in my department that week and fly back to California with my family. Get an attorney and fight my case from there. Only I never made it back to California. There were always speed traps mid-week. Since I was on the run I was always cautious of the little things. That could potentially get us caught. My coworker started picking me up for work since our car was so hot. We couldn't take any extra chances. We woke up late because he wasn't feeling good. So he had to take me. Running late and driving 80+ mph. We ran right into a speed trap and pulled over.

I wasn't worried at all. I told him not to speak for me. My alias hadn't let me down yet. However he didn't have one. When I saw that they were taking him. I gave myself up. It was May 9th of 2009. I had 2 outstanding felony warrants, and I had absconded from my Rehab Program. I was praying that I would not be sent to prison. But most likely I would be. He called his mama before they cuffed him, so that she could come and get the car. I called my job letting them know I would not be in that day. It was bound to happen. There was no way around being caught. Although, I had some hope that I could make it five years. I knew deep down inside that. That was unrealistic. This was actually a perfect time to be arrested. I was clean and I could start my life over from this moment on. As much as I claimed to be ready to see the judge. I was still very terrified. Now I had no choice. I was cuffed in the back seat of a police truck right next to my lover. I cried not just because I was going to jail. But because God had finally answered my prayers, along with death I had prayed many times to be caught. I knew it was the only way to end the life that I was living.

I closed my eyes and leaned my head back. I could feel the body heat of my lover. This gave me some comfort but one thing I knew for

Tamekia Nicole

sure was that we were done. It was over and after this I would move on. Hopefully he would too. It hurt my heart to know that we both had cheated ourselves out of a life worth living. We both cheated ourselves out of good health and stability. When I look back, the partying wasn't worth it. None of it allowed us to amount to anything.

We were un-cuffed and booked into Clark County Detention Center. I wiped my tears and hugged him one last time. We sat in an open room full of other criminals waiting to be processed. I waited so long, that I fell asleep. I was awakened by the sound of his voice telling me that it would be okay and no more tears. With a heavy heart I called my mom and told her that I had been arrested and I may be going to prison. She listened and told me to call her when I knew for sure. I hung up the phone. I was scared and emotional. I was saddened the most at the thought of what I was putting my mom through. As the oldest I had let her down; and my pain and struggle wasn't just mine. I was so selfish that I never recognized that until it was too late.

I made a few more calls from the holding tank. I called our house and my job to let them know the full story. I wasn't surprised that they fully supported me and were willing to do anything to help me thru my situation. At 9 in the morning the holding tank was pretty peaceful. But I knew that soon it would be filled up with battered women, prostitutes, killers, drunk drivers and transients. So I found a resting spot away from toilet but facing the mounted T.V. I knew that I wouldn't be going upstairs for about 48 hours. Vegas county jail was always packed. But what else was to be expected in a 24 hour town, where they gave you a long leash to fuck up....but when they caught you that leash turned into a choker. I went upstairs in record time less than 48 hours. I was settled into my housing unit and I would be seeing the judge in a few days for my revocation hearing. "Hang em High Mosley," that was my judge, and he didn't give any chances. Probation was your only chance. I sat on my bunk and looked around my pod. There were a few faces that I recognized including C.O.'s.

My job sent my final check to the jail. It was close to a thousand dollars, as well as some extra money along with a card that everyone signed. I always had support and I was very loveable it showed in the relationships that I kept. It even showed in the relationships that I destroyed.

If only I could use that same charisma on the Judge and my Probation Officer. I just may be able to get out of this legal web I was caught in. My hopes of that was low, realistically I was ready to be done. If I was reinstated, I would have to start the whole song and dance again...the rehab, the reporting to my P.O., and the weekly visits to court for a status check. I would rather just do the time and get on with what was left of my life. My P.O came to see me and discuss what he would be recommending to the Judge. Right when I saw his face I knew I was fucked. This was a brand new P.O. I had no rapport with him so I listened and took notes and prepared myself for the worst. I was looking at revocation in two cases, both gross misdemeanors that had turned into E felonies. Both cases would be a sentence of 12-36 months. Hopefully, if I was revoked my cases would run concurrently and not consecutively.

In the mean time I prepared myself for my revocation hearing. My job wrote a letter on my behalf. Even though my new P.O said there wasn't a chance in hell that he would reinstate me. I still submitted my letters and evidence that I would be able to pay my outstanding court fees. My thoughts were already geared towards life in Prison for at least one year. But if I could not go for the sake of my family especially my mama, I was going to try everything.

07C232327

DISTRICT COURT
CLARK COUNTY, NEVADA

Criminal Drug Court Petition   COURT MINUTES   May 12, 2009

07C232327   In the Matter of the Petition Of Tamekia N Johnson

| May 12, 2009 | 10:30 AM | Bench Warrant Return - DTP | BENCH WARRANT RETURN - DTP Court Clerk: Tristana Cox Heard By: Elliott, Jennifer |

HEARD BY: COURTROOM:

COURT CLERK:

RECORDER:

REPORTER:

PARTIES
PRESENT: DeJulio, Douglas P.   Attorney
Johnson, Tamekia N   Petitioner
Public Defender   Attorney

JOURNAL ENTRIES

- Petitioner present in custody. CHOICES representative present. COURT NOTED, Petitioner is being held on two probation violations without a hearing scheduled at this time. Petitioner stated his probation officer, Pendelton, is recommending revocation. Mr. DeJulio stated he spoke to officer Dilinger who advised Parole and Probation intends to proceed. COURT ORDERED, MATTER CONTINUED two (2) weeks.
5/26/09 10:30 AM STATUS CHECK - DTP

(Actual court documentation)

Tamekia Nicole

I was present and in custody too hear my fate, only for my hearing to be continued in two more weeks. My memory was immediately jogged, realizing that I would be going back and forth with Clark County Judicial System for at least another two weeks. This was going to be rough. Hopefully I would get to see my lover at court. As my co-defendant he should be there except for the case that involved my rehab program. It was only so many jail stories that I could listen too. I was ready to hear what would happen to me and for how long it would be happening. Most of the women were institutionalized, that was one of my biggest fears. Becoming a statistic, I was already half way there as a young black woman and a drug addict.

Reading occupied most of my time along with playing cards. I felt like I was getting dumber by the day. Then anxiety began to overtake my every waking thought. I watched women being sent to prison all around me. They came back from their court dates in despair. Unable to be with their small children or families until their release dates. I saw anguish on the faces of women who thought for certain that they were going home. These women were getting heavy sentences too; 10 years to life. All of a sudden I was terrified. The only thing I had to look forward to was my letters from my lover and my rediscovery of the Bible. In such a time of disparity maybe the promises of the Bible could see me thru my dark nights. God knew I needed him. But had he finally decided to turn his back on me too.

Today was the day that I would learn my destiny. I had prayed until my eyes were drowning in tears and my knees went numb from kneeling on a concrete floor. My future was either going to start today or be post-phoned today. It was all up to the Judge. I had a fresh jail house hair do, my eyebrows were arched to perfection and my county blues had been under my mattress for two days. So my creases were fresh. I looked good but looks weren't going to get me anywhere. I had fucked up and it was time to pay the piper. I was lucky that my original Judge (Hang em High Mosely) was on vacation. So, I had half a chance at beating my cases. With my heart pounding and beads of sweat forming on forehead and upper lip. I felt like I might vomit or pass out or both. I stood when the Judge called my name and when she sentenced me to prison in both my cases. I dropped to my knees and screamed. As tough as I tried to appear, I didn't want to go to prison. I was petrified.

Tamekia Nicole

The only thing I knew about prison is what I seen on T.V and on movies. I could only think that I wouldn't make it out alive. I was so distraught the judge called for a medic to attend to me. I refused to leave the court room. I begged the judge to reconsider. I had my court fees, I had letters of reference and I was begging her to have mercy on me. But she dismissed me. She advised me to take my time in prison to consider my priorities. She said that I was such a beautiful young lady and although my situation was tragic and unfortunate. I needed to get my life together. I stood up and regained my poise and thanked her for her words of advisory. I assured her that I would take head to her words. No words can explain how I felt in that court room on that day. My dignity and pride had long been gone. I knew at that point there would be no escape from what was to be my destiny, which was prison.

I walked back to my pod, in my cuffs and shackles. As I walked in, all my jail buddies were waiting for me to tell them what the Judge had said. But the look on my face told them that my life in a jail cell; wasn't quite over. I let my destiny be determined by my reckless actions and unsavory decisions. Drugs and lack of judgment was sending me packing to a place that housed killers, thieves, and addicts. They don't tell you when you are going to be rolled up and sent off to prison. They don't want anyone blowing up the bus or planning any escapes. But I felt it that night. As soon as I drifted off to sleep a C.O tapped me on my foot and told me it was time. I sat up and looked around, some were sleeping. Some were up waiting to hug those that were off to the next part of their journey. I gave a few hugs and waived as I grabbed my pillow case full of my belongings and headed out the corridor to be transported to Florence McClure Women's Correctional Center.

I sat in the holding tank all night talking with others who were going to be transported. I listened to the stories and made mental notes of the things that I thought I would need to survive. The only thing I knew about prison was what I saw on T.V. I would find out in just a few hours if T.V. was a true depiction of that. They came in like drill sergeants and made us take everything off and bend, squat and cough. The prison guards looked like men. They gave us men jumpsuits to put on and shackled our wrists to our waist, and

Tamekia Nicole

shackled our ankles together. They led us to a white van, with tinted windows. I remember riding down the Las Vegas strip in that van. I pinched myself, still unable to fathom that for the next year I would be in prison. Hopefully being imprisoned would free my mind and release my demons.

Tamekia Nicole

07C232327

DISTRICT COURT
CLARK COUNTY, NEVADA

Criminal Drug Court Petition	COURT MINUTES	June 16, 2009

07C232327   In the Matter of the Petition Of Tamekia N Johnson

June 16, 2009	10:30 AM	Bench Warrant Return - DTP	BENCH WARRANT RETURN - DTP Court Clerk: Tristana Cox Relief Clerk: ELAINE YORK Heard By: Jack Ames

HEARD BY: COURTROOM:

COURT CLERK:

RECORDER:

REPORTER:

PARTIES PRESENT:
DeJulio, Douglas P.	Attorney
Johnson, Tamekia N	Petitioner
Public Defender	Attorney

JOURNAL ENTRIES

- Petitioner present in custody. Mr. DeJulio noted the Petitioner has a revocation hearing set for 6/17. Petitioner stated her probation was revoked and she will be serving 12/36 months in both cases. COURT ORDERED, Petitioner RELEASED on the Drug Court hold ONLY and NOTED Petitioner is unable to participate in the Drug Court Program. Colloquy regarding balance owed to the court. Mr. DeJulio indicated the Petitioner needs to set up payment arrangements upon release. CASE CLOSED.

PRINT DATE: Page 2 of 2   Minutes Date: June 05, 2009

(Actual court documentation)

CHAPTER 35

THE FISH TANK

Tamekia Nicole

There are no welcome mats or trumpets that play when you enter the prison. However there are predators that are awaiting fresh fish, so that can grab ahold of their money and their bodies. I was scared as I watched all the prisoners clear the way for the newbies as we were escorted down the hallway. Our housing unit was known as the *fish tank*. The fish tank is where I would be spending the next four weeks being psychologically evaluated; go to a dentist and an OBGYN. You are locked down for 23 ½ hours a day. You are allowed out for a half an hour to shower and use the phone. You are housed in a cell with 11 other women. I was terror stricken, but I made a promise to myself that I would not cry here. I would do my best not to show weakness. Since I was so emotional I had no idea how I was going to hold up. So I did my best.

I was friendly but not to friendly. I tried to do more observing than talking. I watched how others interacted with each other, and luckily I had a "friend" with me from the county jail and I was sure to see others that I had did county time with. In my room was a little bit of every kind of criminal, a drunk driver, a few probation & parole violators, a violent offender, and a few like me…who had a chance but didn't listen or follow directions. In addition to our room, there was the certified OG who had done two prior stints in prison. Some of us talked about our cases, some of us remained quiet. For the first few days I just tried to keep my composure and make phone calls to the people in my life who mattered, my mama, a few friends, and I even called his mama. Even though my mom said that she was done with me. She promised to be by my side. Tears are streaking down my face as I recall all the pain I heard in her voice. I told her that I had $1,000 on me but I wasn't sure how long that money would last over the course of one year. The last thing I wanted to do was take from her because I couldn't get my shit together.

I loosened up over the next few days and enjoyed the fact that we could see out onto the yard and watch general population. It was so weird looking out windows that were no bigger and wider than your forearm. I watched as the girls on the yard vied for the attention of the certified OG in my room. They wanted to pay her, get her commissary and be her wife. This amazed me. I've always been fascinated with human interactions especially ones that were unfamiliar to me. This was definitely an unfamiliar territory. That would either kill me or make me stronger.

Tamekia Nicole

We talked shit, played cards, made dice outta hardened toilet paper, communicated with chicks on the yard that we knew and passed the time. The second day in the fish tank a C.O. came in and told us that Michael Jackson had passed. I remember all 12 of us singing Michael Jackson songs until we fell asleep. There was a certain amount of nostalgia that covered the room that night. That made you think about what was; what could have been and what was still yet to be. Excitement and fear were the only emotions that ran thru my body.

There were so many questions I wanted to know the answers too. But I kept my mouth closed, I was mindful that I didn't look like anyone and I didn't talk like anyone there and I never wanted to be pointed out as the weak one. You've probably heard stories about prison relationships between the women and prison relationships between the male guards and the women. I will tell you that it's true and I fell into the trap of an unpredictable love affair with the OG in my unit. She slid a note onto my bed late at night that said; "I know you're not gay, but you will see that I am a shark around here and you will want to roll with me." I think I was a little flattered but mostly scared.

I was awake when she slid the note on my bed, but I never opened my eyes. In the morning, she was extra nice and gave me some of her breakfast, since I was probably the greediest one in there. It was a kind gesture since I felt like I was always starving. I got to know her as she did me. I listened to her advice and her stories and what led her to smiley road. I was intrigued by her. She was different, aggressive but with a teddy bear like demeanor. She was stud with a fade, a missing tooth and a bum leg. She shared that her first trip to prison, some years back was because she stabbed her wife a dozen times. The days and nights passed as we were each called out at different times to go to the dentist, see a psychiatrist and get pelvic exams. They took your blood to see if you had the virus or any other communicable diseases. Also so that when you were released you didn't leave with anything that you didn't come in with. This was real life and very similar to what you saw on T.V.

We always gossiped about why some girls went to the OBGYN more than others and who would be lucky enough get new teeth that the state paid for. In hindsight none of it is funny. All those potential

Tamekia Nicole

scenarios could either damage or severely ruin your life. As humans we often joke about the misfortune of others, just to mask the pain that we feel inside, but don't know how to deal with. I was one of them. I went to all my appointments and passed with flying colors, my coochie, teeth, and mental health all got the A-O.K from the doctors. Although, I was hesitant to tell the psychiatrist everything about me I did my best to be honest. I also decided that a good way to pass my time and not get my ass whooped while I was in prison...Was to take the OG up on her offer, to be her wife. I saw how she operated. How she was able to get things smuggled to her, how well respected she was. Plus I could release my sexual frustrations with her. I looked at it more as a survival technique versus a love connection. A decision that I was bound to regret.

I started having the perks of an OG's wife right away. The trustees smuggled razors, Q-tips, a relaxer, magazines and body-wash, in to her and I had privy to all of it. While my cellmates looked at me in awe, I was shaved, smelling good, clean ears and a fresh perm. I was ready to make my debut in general population; looking unfazed by the curve ball life had thrown me. Every day was the same routine in my cell. We ate breakfast around 6am, we went back to sleep, around 11 they let us out for 30 minutes, we ate lunch, took a nap, played cards, ate dinner, lights out, and then every night or at least every other night I was getting head from the OG. She made everyone else turn towards the wall. She ran everything including me. My previous abusive relationships made me such an easy target. Then one by one we stared being called out to start our real prison journey...GENERAL POPULATION. After four weeks of being locked down and no sunlight. I was ready to order from the commissary list, take a long shower, and reap the benefits of having an OG for a girlfriend. As crazy as it seemed I was happy because I knew without one doubt that my next stop would be home whether I remained in Vegas, or went back to California. My time of freedom was coming. I was hoping that my year would fly by.

Tamekia Nicole

General population was loud and a little bit intimidating. The first night that you go to general population you most likely go to A-Pod. A-Pod is the ghetto of all pods it's the transition pod, until they figure out where to permanently house you for the duration of your sentence. The C.O.'s are in and out of A-Pod because shit gets real in there. I saw how real things could get, when I went to go use the phone and saw a girl beat another girls head in with the phone receiver. I figured that this is where 10 years of getting beat up by my lover would separate me. From those who got beat up versus those who did the beating. I just wanted to go home the same way I came in...a pretty face with no cuts or permanent scarring. Not knowing if it that would be a possibility or not, I proceeded every action with caution.

My OG girlfriend had put me up on a lot of game and with her as my woman. This one year would hopefully fly by. Since I had a low level felony there was a likely hood that I would be sent to a low level security camp in Jean, Nevada. My girlfriend also put me up on that because she didn't want me to go. Everybody wanted and needed someone to do their time with. Whether it was inside the prison walls or...Outside the prison walls. I had no one. Since me and my lover could no longer communicate. I did my time with her. Much like when they initially "roll you up" to come to prison. They roll you up to go to camp that same way. No one knows when. They just announce it over the speaker using only your back number. Then the C.O's come and get you. I had been in general population for about two weeks. I was just getting used to being there when I heard my back number announced over the loud speaker.

My girlfriend was right. She also warned me that her last girlfriend, who was sent to prison, came back within 11 days to be with her. I better find a way back before then. Or she would send somebody up there and they would hurt me. I found myself yet again involved in an abusive situation. Although I had seen her aggressive side, I never fathomed being on the other end of her anger. I carefully listened to her for several nights prior to my departure to camp, on how to get sent back to the prison. Even though I didn't really know how I would accomplish being sent back. I had every intention on following her directions step by step. The only

Tamekia Nicole

factor that worked in my favor was that not every low level offender was sent to camp.

At 6am, I was told to roll up for camp. I hoped down from my top bunk and grabbed my stuff. I was irritated and sleepy but I did as I was told. When you go to camp you also had to cough and squat. But this time when I coughed. I had to be extra careful because I had a 14k gold wedding band that my girlfriend had given me. Wrapped in plastic and stuffed inside of me. I had tucked it behind my cervix that way when they demanded those hard, deep coughs I knew it wouldn't be flying out. That ring solidified our union, and I was damn sure supposed to come back with it on my finger. At camp they expected you to fight fires for a dollar a day or pick up trash on the side of the freeway. I had a master plan though I wouldn't be getting hella dirty. I was going to get back to my girlfriend and eat chicken, watch T.V and play cards. I had been sending kites to the psychiatrist and telling him some truths about my emotional state. But mostly lie's so that they would send me back to the women's facility to undergo a psych evaluation. If you are undergoing a psych evaluation you not suitable to be in a low level security facility. That was my plan.

I had sent over a dozen kites to the doctor and finally I heard my back number being called over the loud speaker at camp. We had just finished with orientation and watching a video on fighting fires and what was expected of us. I put my head down while the video played and even when they told me to lift my head up, I didn't. I was exhausted and I was dirty I just wanted to rest. But I hoped up when I heard my back number 1037156, I thought I was going to see the psychiatrist. But I was actually being summoned to the Sergeant's office. I had no fear, my only fear was getting the shit beat out of me if I didn't hurry up and get back. My Bunkie thought I was dumb. But I felt like I had things under control. I went to the Sergeant's office with confidence and I sat down smugly in the chair in front of her desk. She said "Ms. Johnson, we know you have a girlfriend back at the woman's facility," I just sat there with a smirk on my face, and played stupid. She also asked me what did I plan on doing if they didn't send me back...I replied "escape." There were no fences at camp. So it was highly likely that anyone could just walk off. The Sergeant did not like that answer at. Her reply to me was "You're going to Ad-Seg; Ms. Johnson," I asked her

Tamekia Nicole

"Is that the Hole?" She said "Yes." "Roll my shit up then." I made it back to the prison in 38 hours. I beat 11 days.

The hole, I left a low level security prison and went to the hole. On the ride back to the prison in my shackles, I glared out the window at the dry terrain that made up most of Nevada, and I thought to myself...*you sure are dumb, Tamekia.* I came back dirty, exhausted and my Mohawk was awry. As I was being escorted down the hallway, all of general population had to stay behind all red lines. It was a hallway clearance and no movement was allowed. Honestly, I felt like a celebrity, everyone knew whose girlfriend I was. They would make sure that she knew I was back. Every corner we came too I looked frantically to see if she was somewhere in the hallway. I wanted her to see for herself, the level of loyalty that I had towards her. But I didn't see her.

I always imagined the hole being black and noisy. It was noisy but it wasn't dark at all. I was put in a two man cell, with no roommate and handed papers. I now had pending escape charges and a panel would review my case. If I lost I would not only be doing my original sentence, but an additional year from the hole. In the hole you only came out for 15 minutes and your meals were given to you thru a slit in the door. *What have I gotten myself into?* It was too late to turn back. So I made myself comfortable. The view from my room was a junkyard and for the first few days I just peered out the window and slept. I came out to shower and call my mom. But I never told her that I was in the hole. I had caused enough damage.

Finally, they gave me a roommate and she told me not to worry that when my hearing came they would most likely let me out of the hole. Her words did not stop me from worrying. Every time I glanced at my paperwork, I thought about doing a whole year with only 15 minutes out of my cell and NO SUNLIGHT. Then returning to general population to do an additional year...This just might make me fold. But there wasn't shit I could do. The hole was so noisy it was like no one ever slept. Then I noticed that every time different cells were out for their shower time, they went to a door that was adjacent to a pod in general population. They went to this door, knocked on it and then a dozen envelopes were pushed under the

Tamekia Nicole

gap in the door into our pod. I asked my roommate what that was about and she told me that, if you have a girlfriend in general population that's how you write to each other. Wow, I wondered how come I hadn't had any mail.

But if the police catch you, you're not only going to be in trouble, but the other girls were going to be pissed at you for getting their mail confiscated. I had watched long enough, so during my shower time I knocked a special knock and a flood of mail was pushed under the door. I had to look if I had mail. Plus I had to go around and deliver everyone else's mail. I ran around as fast as I could, sliding mail under doors, and calling out names. Not sure who was still in the hole and who had been let out. It was an adrenaline rush. Then I went back to my room and I had at least six letters from my girlfriend. I was happy, excited and glad that she had missed me. Behind prison doors, everybody needed someone even if it was just for that moment. I needed those words of encouragement. I needed guidance from the world that would be my home. I needed to know that there was someone tangible within my reach. That could show me affection. She was that.

The first few letters she was kind of mad wondering why she hadn't heard from me. I wanted to yell out. "Well probably because I didn't know shit about this inmate mail system!" Her letters were heart-warming, romantic and filled with lists of things NOT to tell the police during my hearing. Promises of what she would get me when I was out. I wrote her back letters filled with appreciation and whatever else I felt was appropriate to say. During that quiet time I wrote my mom, my old job, and I even wrote my lover in hopes that his mom would send the letter off for me, to wherever he was at. The hole started to become unbearable it was too much time to think and not enough space to move. One roommate moved out and I was alone with my wayward thoughts until they moved another one in. This roommate was crazy and she was from the Bay, we got along immediately. She wasn't the brightest crayon in the box but she was playful and she made my time go by fast. We stayed up late singing, talking shit, and playing cards. It wasn't all shits and giggles though. We had many nights when we would cry and

Tamekia Nicole

think about the reasons we were locked up like animals and getting meals thru a metal door.

I was now on psych meds and so was my roommate. But she was on the kind that cause severe drowsiness, mine only caused the munchies. Fuck. I would watch her sleep for hours. She hardly ate so I was always able to either get seconds or at least eat her dessert. Then she put me on. By that I mean, she cheeked her meds and gave me half. I would be sleep for at least two days. They called it *getting in the car*. I stayed in the car on and off for the duration of my sentence to the hole. When you're in the car it takes a lot to wake you up. It was a miracle that I heard the other girls screaming my name one afternoon. My girlfriend had pulled some strings. She was in the hole with some of her friends in the laundry department.

I watched with such pride as I she walked up the stairs and stood in front of my window. She told me that I had a pair of jeans, jewelry and a pair of white patent-leather Jordan's waiting for me when I got out. She also reiterated that I don't tell the police shit. I would be out before I knew it. She was right I did 36 days in the hole. I was released me with no new charges. I had impressed my girlfriend beyond belief, by coming back to her so fast. She showered me with everything that you could make you happy in prison. My favorite of all the gifts was the 14k gold necklace with the Jesus piece. It was an amazing feeling. There was a nice little line of other women who were dying to be in my place with her. I never imagined being so elated in a place that was so dark. I was like her trophy. We found happiness in the moments that we shared together. Everyone else saw it. We were a very popular couple. But because of her outward appearance, and our age difference... A lot of people also wondered why and how we were a couple.

There were still a lot of things that according to her that I needed to be taught. When she made that statement I started thinking...this may be more than I can handle. With nowhere to run, the only option was the Police. That never sounds good.

CHAPTER 36

RULES

Tamekia Nicole

You may think that it sounds funny. There were so many rules to being the girlfriend of an OG Stud. At first everything was good. I was getting head on a regular basis, eating chicken (chicken cost a lot on commissary,) sleeping on her air mattress when the guards weren't trippin'. She put $100 extra dollars on my books every month. I had jewelry, jeans (mostly lifers were the only ones with jeans or other OG's), and everyone respected and spoke to me. I was like a prison celebrity by association.

But not everyone liked me. My girlfriend was wanted. Other women wanted her, they wanted to put money on her books, do her laundry, and bring her food. Honestly, those gestures used to piss me off. But I had to learn that there were rules everywhere, especially here. You fail to follow the rules of State Prison, it could cost you. For the most part, others either knew me as her girlfriend, or the pretty girl with the Mohawk. It didn't make me a bit of difference. Prison relationships in my experience often carry into life after prison. The thought had crossed my mind. I was in such a vulnerable state, and excessively needy. I strongly considered being with her on the outside. Just switch it up....and then I had a taste of her violent side. There was no way that I was going to commit to another abusive situation.

It started off as little statements she would say to me, or small gripes here and there. She was very particular about her way of life in prison. She liked powder on her sheets, when they were fresh out of the dryer. On particular days of the week, especially when it was hot, she loved orange soda. She liked coffee or hot chocolate to be brought to her while she played dominoes on the yard on Sunday mornings. She liked you to sit next to her during card games and not speak unless spoken too. But then again, she loved when I spoke. She loved to listen to my stories about my life. She loved the way I articulated my words. Some of the rules were taught to me, and some she got really pissed when I didn't already know. It was frustrating. How in the fuck was I supposed to know to put powder on her sheets? Who was I supposed to ask? The biggest rule that was hard for me to understand and follow was not speaking. I was talking before I was doing anything else in life.

Under no circumstance, do you speak to other studs, or soft studs, out of her presence. It was a sign of disrespect, especially if it was a popular or OG stud. The more I tried not to speak to certain people, the

Tamekia Nicole

more they spoke to me. It was so nerve racking. Those who were disrespectful and spoke to me knew what they were doing, they knew the rules. There was a particular soft stud with a cut across her face. She used to flirt with me from the window, when I was in the fish tank. She was from San Francisco, she was loud, wild and foul. She was chocolate, thick and the cut across her face gave her a certain sex appeal. She was forbidden for me to speak too. But sometimes I couldn't help it. She was hilarious and would be so loud that if she did something I would laugh. Even laughing was considered speaking and disrespectful. My girlfriend always knew when there was even the slightest interaction with the soft stud. She would cuss me out. Sometimes it hurt my feelings. I didn't want to fight with her. But sometimes I just didn't give a fuck.

We started arguing a lot. My circle of friends insisted that I leave her alone. I had considered breaking it off, but I had so much fear pumped in me that it never seemed like the right time. So the shit that I could brush off I did. The other stuff I just held it in. One time I didn't pack the frozen chicken the right way in her bed side cooler. While I was out on the yard she threw the wet soggy box of chicken on my bed….everything was wet. Nobody said shit to her about it. Not even the Police. There were certain ways that you cook in there. All the cooking is done in the microwave. The food preparation is very important. Somehow someone touched her food without my knowledge. I kept on cooking and when her food was done I brought it to her. She wouldn't eat it. She threw it in the garbage and told me that I owed her money. She checked me in front of her clique…her niece and her best friend. There were other trivial things that she blew up about. But there wasn't really shit I could do.

There weren't just rules with her, there were prison rules period. You never ask another inmate about their case. That may have been the number one rule. I was nosey though. So sometimes my girlfriend knew the scoop and sometimes she would get mad that I asked her. I slept two or three beds down from Kelly Ryan, she appeared on the show "Snapped," her and her husband were world known body builders. They were convicted of kidnapping, arson, and the murder of their assistant. There were several other high profile cases that were either housed in my pod or in the facility.

Tamekia Nicole

It was a little scary walking around with convicted killers. There was the pretty black girl, who shot an AK-47 at the police they gave her 40 years to life. Her girlfriend used to beat the shit out of her. I used to ask my girlfriend why they stayed, in those situations. Of course it was none of my business.

You never ran to the police, which was pretty much the same as on the streets. Some people followed the rule of not talking to or befriending any women that were convicted of killing their baby. My Bunkie was a baby killer. I loved the shit out of her and I never knew that she really killed her baby until I googled it when I got out. She was on OG even though her conviction was the worst kind I was allowed to talk to her. She was a soft stud that was known for liking and spoiling black women. The rules were the rules, and you followed them or you were fucked up. I'm not sure what rule I had broken, but the time that me and my girlfriend had as a couple was aggressively coming to an end. I just remember that it was late at night, more like early morning. It was about 3am, and she came and woke me up and told me to get up. I told her no, that it was late and I had group in the morning. She said "Either get your ass in this bathroom, or you're going to the hospital and I am going to the hole." Needless to say I got my ass up.

She directed me to the last stall, the biggest one...the handicap stall. She stood across from me on the back wall and I stood on the wall, adjacent to the next stall. Although her exact words are a blur right now, I know that she said something like, "you bet not cry." She socked me in my stomach and choked shoved me. A small stream of blood trickled down the left side of my neck. One solitary tear fell from my eye. I had to make sure that the collar of my tee shirt covered it up or the police would sure to be asking questions. That was the last thing that I needed. Whether or not I followed or broke these rules, my girlfriend was so aggressive and volatile all the time. I was relieved when she broke up with me. I was so tired of catering to her. Yes I was a pleaser, but in all reality I was supposed to be there working on my criminal characteristics. After we broke up, she would still get an attitude with me her bullshit that technically did not fall under the umbrella of her concerns. But yet another rule was, once I was hers, I would always be hers.

Tamekia Nicole

When we broke up, I became a ghost on the yard. People, who once broke their neck to speak to me, looked right passed me. People bumped into me more often. Dirty looks were everywhere I turned. There was even a time when someone came up to me, questioning about bullshit. I never buckled. My ex tried to take a pair of leather New Balances back from me, but I wouldn't take them off my feet. She ran up, we were chest to chest, I never bucked and she did not get those shoes back. I stayed indoors for two weeks, only going outside to get my meals. I was miserable and the fact that I was in prison was taking a toll on me. I made myself miserable because instead of getting rehabilitated I had fallen for another abuser.

I broke the rule and started talking to Scarface. The chocolate soft stud. We were broke up so I thought it was cool. Or maybe I was just looking for some sexual gratification. When my ex found out, she let me know that I could leave prison with something I didn't come in with. She was referring to HIV one of her close friends had it. I was terrified it was about four months until my first eligible date to go home. There was other bullshit rules… don't sit your ass at a card, domino, or pinochle game and not know how to play. A lot of times girls were gambling, or you were playing "rise and fly." Nobody wanted to loose and honestly since more than 50% of the population were doing more than just a few years, there was a lot of anger and tension built up. So anything that may seem minor to you was major to them.

I stopped breaking all those punk ass rules and just enjoyed my last few months. I knew I needed to spend the remaining time I had there clear of anything that would potentially get me killed. I took heed to all those rules and prison life became a little easier. Good thing I took head to those rules, because I was in an honor dorm called the Arch Program, where you went to groups all day long from 7:30 to 3:30pm that focused on recovery. I needed to concentrate on that so I could have as many tools under my belt as possible to remain drug free once I was released. It was good program that also had a lot of rules, and there were particular jobs that each person was assigned. There was a rotation of several different jobs. If you did not do your job correctly you were subject to punishment including being kicked out of the program.

Tamekia Nicole

I got a lot out of the program and I had a lot of heart to hearts with the director of the program. I studied the material and applied the homework assignments to real life situations I had or anticipated having. There was a comradery in the program that was similar to sisterhood. It was far from perfect, we were in prison, but we also were all in there trying to reach the same goals...sobriety, and staying out of the system.

There were so many women that were institutionalized. I saw it in their actions, the way they spoke and when I knew that this wasn't their first trip to prison. It was heartbreaking and I didn't want to be like them. I never thought that I was better than anyone however I did know that a lot of my upbringing and childhood circumstances was better than more than half of the women there. That makes a difference. Life isn't Rocket Science but it is Psychology. My time ticked further and further down and I had less problems. I worked my program that is until I was kicked out. Remember I told you about rules and punk ass rules. I got caught up in a punk ass rule. Over a card game with a convicted killer, it was true that I wasn't the best Spade's player but it was also true that the women with long sentences did punk ass shit to get short timers sent to the hole.

Since my time was winding down and my patience with the whole prison life was paper thin, I didn't give a fuck and if I had to go home from the hole I would. She was talking to much shit that night, and her partner was the Scarface soft chocolate stud. My partner was my buddy L Dog. I did something wrong and the killer, started talking shit to me. I talked shit right back. She threw down her cards, and I had to remind her that she was just a stone cold killer she had killed that girl by accident. It was all over a pimp. The killer had been picked on and started carrying a knife with her and stabbed the girl accidently during a confrontation. At that point I had already been threatened to be infected with HIV. I planned on beating the dog shit out of this *killer*.

We didn't do anything but bark at each other, but my body language let her know that my bark damn sure matched my bite. Even though we didn't physically fight, I was kicked out of the honor dorm and sent to the adjacent pod 9B. That was considered the ghetto. 9B was the 24/7 house party. The C.O's didn't care, and you better know how to fight because if anything jumped off, the police would not break it up.

Tamekia Nicole

So off to 9B I went. My next stop was home anyway. Fuck Smiley Rd. and its rules. I only had 30 days and a wake up. My year was damn near over. Just don't fuck with me and I won't fuck with you was my mentality.

CHAPTER 37

BUTTERFLY DOORS

Tamekia Nicole

My release date was around the corner. I barely slept because I dreamt of life out of here, away from a life that I never want to see again. The feeling of being caged like an animal is so cruel, and so cold. There is no escape you literally have to grin and bear it. I had grinned, I had even cried but I bared it and I had long been ready to go.

I started making phone calls with the last little bit of money I had and let certain people know that I was coming home. There were so many surprise letters, cards and money put on my books from people who I thought forgot about me. I wanted to get a jump start on doing the next write thing. I called my mom and told her as soon as they approve my half way house I would call her back. I heard her happiness and relief thru the phone. That's my mama, she had my back. She sent mail and cards every week and she sent me her hard earned money. It's hard to explain the exact relationship that I have with my mama, but I know that she loves me and I love her way more then she could ever imagine. My halfway house took about two weeks to approve and it cost $700, I had to put all of that together from a pay phone. Nothing in there was free. You better have it, fuck with someone who has it, or know how to get it. Luckily, I had it. I wasn't ballin by far...but I never wanted for much. Blessings were pouring down on me, a very good friend that hadn't heard from me found me and not only wrote me, but put in more than half for my release to the halfway house. My mama paid the other half.

They took my exist blood and approved my release to the halfway house in the same week. Exit blood means they are done with you; they've compared your current blood to your blood test when you came in. If it all looks the same, you're ready to go thru the coveted butterfly doors. Those doors are the doors that separate you from tangible and intangible. I was ready. Although things had previously been tense, with my ex-girlfriend and Scarface, I made peace with them. You never know what situations you may find yourself in later on down the line and the bottom line is...even if I had no intentions to consistently keep in contact with them, these were women that I had built some type of relationship with. Making peace is always good but only if it's genuine. My any my ex, talked for days in a row leading up to my release and I remember before we actually spoke her girlfriend told me it was okay. I looked at her girlfriend early on a Sunday, and asked her to take off her glasses so I could see her eyes, and let her know that when I was ready to talk to my ex, I would…I wasn't ready yet. It was nice talking to her on the yard, away from everybody. All the busy bodies, gossip mongers and haters.

She gave me advice on staying clean and doing things for myself and to never speak to my lover again. She was right; she was giving me game that I should have been applying to my life years ago. But I was still living and I was for damn sure still learning. We talked about writing each other and how I would send pictures. She asked me not to forget about her and I told her that I could never. I told her not to beat that poor girlfriend of her to death. She laughed that missing tooth laugh, which only she could laugh. She was a barracuda but had a few teddy bear characteristics.

I had a long therapy session with the director of the Arch Program. Even though I had been kicked out of the honor dorm, I requested to see her and it was granted. Sure I picked up a lot of prison game that could be essential to surviving in the streets; I need therapeutic advice to keep the demons away that came with fighting an addiction. At that time I had been clean 1 year & 5 months. She was such wonderful genuine lady and she directed the program from an honest and genuine place in her heart. It touched me and I listened to every word she said. I was honest with her and she was honest about believing that I could and would make it. Saying goodbye wasn't tough, but it surreal. Women who I could never being connected or exposed to, became a part of my life and a lot of nights parts of my prayers. Prison is tough, it's not staged to look rough for cinematic purposes when you see shows like "Locked Up." If you are serious about changing it will change you. My heart hurt for the ladies serving life without parole. My heart hurt for the people who hadn't come to terms with the change that needed to be made within their selves. My heart hurt for those who had no family support and depended on other inmates to help take care of them once they got out.

Crazy emotions stirred inside me my very last night on Smiley Rd. I thought about my lover and what was going on with him. The whole entire year that I was in prison, I only talked to his mama once and that was when I was in the fish tank. Although our relationship was far from perfect, I felt totally abandoned by his family. I called a few times with my calling card and no one ever answered.

Tamekia Nicole

What no one knew but me and God was that I prayed for a separation from my lover, and I would take that in any form that God gave it to me in. Prison was my way out. Prison was the time when I could get comfortable with my shadow and tested the boundaries in which I was the strongest. Prison made my skin just a little thicker. I have yet to know if that was a good thing or a bad thing. I am still searching for the balance in between passive and aggressive.

The morning came and so did joy. I was called over the loud speaker by my back number...I was stepping back into the world with everything to prove. I grabbed a manila envelope with my letters, pictures, cards, and phone numbers in it and my paperback Bible and walked towards the sunshine. I had to go thru the yard and that when I saw my ex, and everyone else. There wasn't ever supposed to be hugging between inmates and I hugged my ex. We exchanged I love you's, I looked back once....she was still there waving. I waived back. Once all of us where loaded into the van, the butterfly doors were opened up and we drove thru. I watched the butterfly doors close and I took a good look at the prison from the outside. That was an image I never wanted to see again. Maybe I had been scared straight.

CHAPTER 38

THE AFTERMATH

Tamekia Nicole

Getting out of prison in the literal sense is the easiest part. Staying out and getting pieces of your life back is the hardest. I was going to a halfway house and I would be on parole for six months. Any contact with any law enforcement agencies could be an automatic parole violation and send me back. All the passengers in the van were unloaded and un-cuffed in front of the Parole & Probation Department and set free. The first thing I did was walk to the 7-11 across the street and buy a Red Bull, a pack of Marlboro Menthol 100's, and a pack of Big Red Gum. I sat by the flagpole in front of the parole office, cracked open my drink and lit a cigarette. That, was too much excitement, I started getting dizzy. I had to remind myself that there would be plenty time to take everything in. That was the stem of my previous problems....I rushed everything.

The driver for the halfway house pulled up and I jumped in. I was on my way to the Covenant of Love. It was the newest one out of all of the houses that the owner had. It was very nice. There were two or three to a room. Most of those women I had known, either from doing county time with them or state time. I had no intentions on staying in this house longer than necessary. There was a 10pm curfew, chores, house meetings, morning-prayer sessions, and mandatory attendance to church and it was clear on the other side of town. Those weren't bad things at all, but my goal was to follow the plan I had come up with. I was now an ex-felon that factor alone would make a difference if I let it.

I had a game plan, and I executed it the first night. But not before I took a long look at myself in a rear mirror. There are no real mirrors in prison. I was okay with what I saw. I saw a bare-face, and a renewed soul looking back at me. I smiled at my own reflection. That was a reward within itself. Some of my housemates were going to Walmart and I jumped in the van with them. I bought a cell phone from a dude that lived at one of the other house locations for $35. It was already activated. I called my mom and let her know that I was out. I called my sister and my best friend. Everyone was so happy to hear my voice and I was happy to hear theirs as well.

Tamekia Nicole

I bought hygiene products, a new bra, panties, Capri jeans, a tee shirt, a perm, lip-gloss, flip flops, and a hoodie. I never wanted to see those prison clothes again. It was late when we came back from Walmart and I took a shower and went to sleep. I slept hard, I remember having vivid dreams and waking up with more positivity then I went to sleep with. Next on the agenda, was to call the job I was on my way to the morning I was arrested to see if I could come reapply. When I called they wanted me to start the next day. I told them that for the first 10 days you are not allowed to leave the house, unless it was for legal business. I was told not to worry that nothing would change in 10 days. I was more than welcome to come back. I was off to a good start. I didn't request to be excused from the 10 day rule. Instead I took my own advice. I rested and didn't rush anything. I applied for medical benefits at the Social Service Office; they gave me general aid, and food stamps. There was food that was shared in the house but with that many people. I wanted to make sure that I had the highest chance of eating what I wanted, when I wanted to eat it. Food was one of the biggest desires I wanted to get back too. I wanted to enjoy food without worrying about a bell ringing to dismiss me.

I prayed every day and every night. I lead prayers in our morning meetings. I had no desire to use drugs but I did have a small desire to talk to my lover. I think it was natural for me to want to know about his status. I had no idea if he was in or out. I had no current phone number for his mama, but I was able to reach her at her job. She still worked the graveyard shift at the gas station She agreed to meet up with me, so that I could get whatever belongings hadn't been stolen by his sister in law and the side chick. We had lunch that day as well. She caught me up on my lover's whereabouts and his status. He still had one more year to do. That was a perfect amount of time to get my shit together. Whether I waited for him or not a year was perfect. She also told me that soon after we were arrested the bank foreclosed on the house. So she moved into a one bedroom by herself and refused to ever live with any one of us again. In my head I was thinking… I didn't say shit about living with you and I will never be asking you for any type of housing assistance. At that moment I recognized that his mama was a trigger for me. She would be an unnecessary stress factor that could send me over the edge. No thank you.

I saw her a few more times and retrieved very few of my belongings. My wardrobe had been ransacked. There were many articles of clothing missing and pairs of shoes. I was used to it. I wasn't even mad or surprised. This had become the norm for me since I had lived in Vegas. But this time I loved myself more than the stolen clothes, I was trying to recover. I also wasn't so concerned with her approval of my life. She gave me my lover's address. I called her every two weeks or so to check on her. That was the extent of our relationship. Even with barely any contact I was jeopardizing my sobriety and my sanity. I still hadn't let go of the sense of loyalty that I felt like I owed her. We did a lot of foul things and put her in danger that she did not deserve. You have to be honest with yourself, and now that I was clean it was imperative that I followed that mantra. Being honest hadn't always been easy for me. But I was going to do my best to start being honest at all costs.

Going back to work was the best way to spend my time. I walked for over 30 minutes to get to the bus stop every morning. I rode one bus for an hour and 15 minutes. During those morning rides, I thought about my life. I thought about my lover's life, and I thought about the lives we both ruined with our dysfunction. Those thoughts made me cry, but those thoughts gave me the drive I needed to push every day. My sales game at work was getting better and better. It was almost like I had never left. I picked up where I left off. I renewed my work friendships and I made new ones. Those friendships saw me thru my tough days. Increased my money and allowed me to see things in myself that I had long forgotten. I started bringing home checks every week that had commas in them. That was always the goal...to be in commission. It was $12 and hour versus commission. Whichever one was higher is what your check would be. The competitor in me refused to do anything but be the best. My best friend at work became my best friend in life. He showed me ways to improve my sales pitch. He showed me how to stack my money. He showed me how to believe in myself, even when no one else did. Then ultimately my coworker became my roommate. It wasn't hard saying bye to the ladies at the halfway house. I had paid my dues there and hopefully I had been an example to them. I followed the rules and my game plan was to just make that a pit stop. I was proud of myself. No one was going to give you anything and I knew that. So I went out and acquired the things I wanted.

With a solid best friend money in the bank, and a new lease on life... I made preparations to move back to California. Not only was my best friend amazing but his girlfriend was as well. Then there was three, me, him and her. We worked together, played together and lived together.

Although they are close to 10 years younger than me, they exposed me to positivity and showed me how to have fun. I let loose and I never felt guilty about it. I even took a trip to see the jack rabbit in Atlanta.

Atlanta was good to me; the jack rabbit was good to me. He cooked for me, and made me feel like a princess. At that moment every bit of love that I ever had for him, came back. I think out of all the interactions we had over the years, that was the only time that we ever loved each other, with the same exact intensity. But just like my other intimate interactions, I was too damaged to move forward. I needed to fix myself first before I could expect a man to fully commit to me. I appreciated him, loved him and continued to prepare for the rest of my life. My lover was in my heart and we stayed in constant contact. I sent money every two weeks, packages, cards, pictures and accepted all his calls. I was still trying to see where my head was at. Plus trying to come to a firm decision about where we stood. Could our relationship be fixed after he came home? It was hard for me to consider letting him go. But it would be even harder going backwards. It was my life and I was learning to not let guilt trips effect decisions that needed to be made.

But until I made my final decision, I was still his and he was still mine. I did what he asked of me. I checked on his mama, I visited other people in his family. Making sure that my visits were in correlation with when he would call. His brother was in and out of the hospital. Even though he couldn't stand me, I gave him my support. When you're loyal even the most detrimental situations, you will find that your loyalty has no expiration date. I was as honest as I could be with my lover but I was mindful to not hurt is feelings and bring him down. He was in the last stretch of his sentence, but I had to mention moving back to California. I needed him to understand that Vegas wasn't good for me, and although location had nothing to do with my frame of mind...I learned in my stints in rehab that I had to change my people, places and things.

He was not happy at the thought of me leaving. But I chose to be selfish. Then I looked back at my 6 years there. I reflected on all the prayers I begged God to answer and that is when I knew that I had to leave. My best chance at surviving and staying clean was to leave him while he was still locked up. Some may think that was a coward move, but I knew it was a safe decision and the best one for my life. It hurt me to tell him that I needed to be with my family. Although I loved him, I was going

Tamekia Nicole

to do what was best for me. He was given the choice to join me after he finished his sentence. But I would not pressure him either way. I wanted to live. I finally had the momentum I needed to do something different and to feel good about my own life decisions.

I never want to inflict pain on anyone in my life especially someone who I had spent a decade with. I just wanted peace. I wanted to be happy and if I couldn't be happy with him. Then I would continue to pursue happiness by myself and with whom-ever else wanted those same things.I contacted my in-law that I had hired at my job and I made peace with her. I apologized for doubting her loyalty and she said that she was proud that I chose to move on without my lover. She had her own dysfunction along with four kids. So I valued those words. I no longer needed or was looking for validation, for the moves that I was making. I just wanted to be home with my family. I wanted and needed my own mama to hug me and tell me that she was proud that I was her daughter. Those were necessities to me. My lover had lost his number one spot, and it was both of our faults. Saying good bye to Vegas and the healthy relationships that I was leaving behind tugged at my heart strings. But see when you are really for someone and their happiness, at some point you may have to say goodbye. I had acquired two best friends and several other people that remain pivotal factors in my growth. That was what life was about. Growing, changing, and maturing.

I said good bye, it was hard…actually it was beyond hard but I knew that the next part of my journey needed to be in California. My lover called the day before my big move. I cried to him and told him that this was best. He sounded more like the man I had once fell in love with. He was drug free and dealing with life circumstances the best he could from where he was at. He could not change my decision and he knew that. I prayed that his new lease on life extended past the prison walls.

CHAPTER 39

HOME SWEET HOME

Love Made Me Do It

Tamekia Nicole

I am in awe that there was so much pain & anguish that I tolerated. But I am more in awe; that I managed to extinguish most of that pain once I left him behind. I belittled myself and justified everything just to show him that I was a loyal woman. Loyalty has no expiration date but if a person is not loyal to you, then your actions are truly in vain. I could have done things better and different and didn't. But as the man, and the head of our relationship he consistently led me to danger. Even though, he had the power to lead us to greatness.

People often ask me if I could change the situations I was entangled in, would I? I am a firm believer that our individual paths are predestined. Everything I went thru was pretty much how it should have been. Everyone serves a purpose in life. Maybe my purpose will be to teach and give others hope, when they think there is no way out, and all is lost. I cried like a baby at the airport but we all knew that I had to go. Similar to a baby bird going out to feed for the first time alone…They had to trust that nature had taken its course. I was rehabilitated and well enough to leave the nest. I felt ready. I was ready to love the people that were still by my side, the right way. I prayed that my love would be reciprocated. Everyone was so elated to see me. I was overwhelmed with emotions, and I felt complete. My mom slept in the bed with me for my first few days and rubbed my hair and just stared at me. I am her first born and her only daughter. She held me and told me how much she loved me. When I tried to apologize for being a family embarrassment she held me even tighter. That was real. This was family and I never wanted to be in a space that took me away from the love that would always be there.

It was good to be home, but honestly it felt foreign to me. Streets looked different, some people were different. But it was okay because I was also different. Change is a part of life. I immediately tried to jump back into the lives of my friends and even that took time. Trust had been lost and everyone's life had continued to evolve. I did my best to respect that. I had burned bridges and told many lies. I prayed that in time, I would be part of the evolving of those that I loved. I left my mama's house after about a week and moved in with my Granny. The last time she seen me I said I would be right back. I never came back. It had been five years. That still makes me cry, I can't believe I left like that. I'm sure she waited up and looked out the windows and the front door…To see if I was coming up the walkway. My Granny is

Tamekia Nicole

someone who never ever failed me, and yet I failed her. Nonetheless, she was happy to see me. She blessed me with a car and talked to me about going back to school. She also told me, I had to improve my work ethic because she wouldn't be around forever to take care of me. I took every piece of her advice and enrolled in school the next day.

My lover got out a little sooner than anticipated. Although I took his calls, and told him I loved him...it was over. I wouldn't allow any fresh starts to stale news. Much to my dismay, he was drunk the very first day he got out. This hammered the nail into the coffin. Ensuring, that we could never be. Prison hadn't changed him. But most definitely, prison had changed me. I could never live the life; that I lived with him ever again. I broke the chains on all my addictions. Including the need to be in his life. Looking back I think about my three failed suicide attempts, the thousands of dollars I spent on getting high; and all my other destructive behavior and I know that I survived for a greater purpose. That has yet to be revealed to me. Starting over in more ways than one. I was eager to start repairing what I could. Some relationships I was able to repair; and some would only exist in my heart. I've learned that I have to be accountable for the roles I played in every situation. I never ever claimed to be innocent, but I can honestly say that my addiction prohibited my ability to function at a normal capacity. My addiction and my perception of love cost me things; that all the money in the world could never recover. I anxiously, anticipate and wait for my karma because no matter what...you reap what you sow.

I came home to stockpiled bills from the IRS and EDD that exceeded 20k. But I also came home, knowing that I had acquired skills that gave me the ability and the mindset to conquer every responsibility I left behind. What else could I ask for, without being greedy? So I take the good with the bad and I deal with it. A lot of prayer, therapy, love and support from my family and friends see me thru every dark hour I have. I try my best every day to be better than I was the day before. Do I fall short? Absolutely. Do I have days that I spend in bed and cry and reflect on the things I have done wrong? Of course. But those bad days don't really come around like they used too. Whether it's a bad day or a wonderful day; I get up and do what is asked of me.

Tamekia Nicole

I hold no shame, but I do carry the guilt of knowing I had a hand in bringing misery to others. I have been judged by so many and I have no control of someone else's perception of my actions. But I learned to be okay with who I see in the mirror. We all sin differently, and my sin is no greater than those who choose to be judgmental. God will deal with me accordingly. I just pray that he has mercy on my soul and that heard my many cries to be forgiven. Ultimately, my lover married the in-law that I hired. The rumors where true, the lies weren't lies. So his step niece is now is wife. His cousin is the one that called and told me. That wasn't to be disloyal, but because I had been around for more than a decade, he thought I should know. It does hurt to know that I played a starring role, in being a fool in my own life. But I let that go too.

Everyone isn't for everyone. As shady as it is that he married someone that I considered a friend. I've accepted that too. I find solace in knowing that I left him first. I knew that I had no room for garbage in my life. I only had room for growth. Every January 19th I acknowledge the fact that I kicked a drug habit that damn near put me six feet under. Every April 21st I acknowledge the fact that I spent one year of my life enclosed in prison. Every day I thank God that I have a chance to really live, to really love and to give myself a chance to create a life worth living. Surviving isn't living, it's merely getting by. I always wanted to do more than just get by. If you've supported me thru out this journey and read my blogs and now my book...I thank you from the bottom of my heart. I realize that I can be sensitive and emotional, but please continue to give me support in the rawest form. I need consistent and constant doses of what is right. I am human and with all the trials and tribulations that I have overcome, sometimes it takes me a little while for it to sink in...I am living proof that everything is possible if you want it bad enough. I was a crack head, a liar, a thief, a criminal and I manipulated men to get money for my habit. But today and every day, I work towards being the change I want to see.

I'm on the right side of the law. I've been clean for almost six years, and I realize that my body is a temple and I don't have to let men use it as a doormat. I am still working on my boundaries with men and I suspect that with time, someone special will come into my life...but first I must fully grasp the concept of SELF LOVE.

Tamekia Nicole

Life isn't easy, but let my story serve as a template on what not to do. Love didn't make me do anything, because that was never love. It was me being complacent and my addiction magnified my fear of being alone. But now that I'm rid of my demons, I realize I was never alone. There were, and are so many people that love me.

Love starts, and ends with you.

Finally…I part with who I was, in order to meet who I have yet to become.

Tamekia Nicole

Dearest Tamekia,

As you look back on life and how it used to be; make sure it's only a glance that serves as a reminder that there is no need to be ashamed of who you were. There is no longer any need to hide from your past; it's where you've been that gives you the strength to battle each day. There is an abundance of greatness inside of you, and now is your time to shine. Although bits and pieces of you are still a work in progress. You have a light that will progressively get brighter and attract the right type of people. Be patient and kind to yourself, you've been thru enough. God has blessed you with something wonderful, and that's the ability to be able to love without reflecting on how many times you have been hurt. However, please keep in mind, that it's imperative that you save some of that love for yourself. It's impossible to love anyone else until you really love you. There is no need to feel insecure, with or without makeup, you are beautiful. Your flaws are what make you unique. These are qualities that cannot be duplicated. They are yours, much like a fingerprint. Be yourself at all times, because everyone else is already taken. There is no longer a need to hide behind sunglasses because you have a black eye that you're trying to conceal, and no need to wear long sleeves or apply make-up to cover up bruises that trail your body. You are free to smile because your soul and spirit are no longer consumed by drugs or an abusive man. I promise that you will never be dragged to a mirror and told that you are ugly. I also promise that your body is not a resting place for men that have no purpose and serve no purpose in your life. Tamekia, my dear Tamekia, I am beyond proud that you are finally on your way to evolving into what everyone already believed you could be but you were unable to see, because you were blinded by what you perceived love to be. Finally, be mindful of your actions, be ready for judgment, steer clear of negative energy and never apologize for being who you are. Anyone who minds your change will never matter and the people that matter will love, that you loved yourself enough to change.

Love Made Me Do It

Tamekia Nicole

Love Made Me Do It

Tamekia Nicole

Tamekia Nicole

Sometimes, you just have to bare it all…in order to recreate the best version of yourself and gain more than you've ever had…

If you or someone you know is a victim of domestic violence. I urge you to get help. Don't allow your fears of being alone take away years of your life. Domestic violence situations affect not only you, but those around you. Love yourself enough to know that love is not violent. Love is merciful, kind, patient and loyal.

If you don't have anyone that you feel you can turn too, please contact <u>The National Domestic Violence Hotline at 1-800-799-7233</u>.

Be kind to yourself and make sure that others are kind to you as well. You only get one chance at life. Don't relinquish your power to someone else. Learn to recognize the early signs of abuse.

ABUSE OCCURS

- Physical
- Sexual
- Emotional

TENSION-BUILDING

- Abuser starts to get angry
- Minor incidents of abuse begin
- Communication breaks down
- Victim feels the need to keep the abuser calm
- Tension becomes too much
- Victim/family members feel like they are "walking on egg shells"

RECONCILIATION/ MAKING-UP

- Abuser apologizes for abuse, promises it won't happen again
- Blames victim for provoking the abuse
- Denies the abuse took place or says it wasn't as bad as the victim claims
- Gives gifts to the victim

CALM

- Abuser acts like the abuse never happened
- No abuse is taking place
- Some promises made during the reconciliation/making-up phase are being met
- Victim hopes the abuse is over

221

Tamekia Nicole

The End